MUSIC ON MARS

MUSIC
ON **MARS**

Why Creativity Is Tomorrow's Critical
Ability, and How to Develop Yours Today

NEIL MOORE

LIONCREST
PUBLISHING

MUSIC ON MARS
Why Creativity Is Tomorrow's Critical Ability,
and How to Develop Yours Today

FIRST EDITION

ISBN   978-1-5445-4832-6 *Hardcover*
        978-1-5445-4831-9 *Paperback*
        978-1-5445-4833-3 *Ebook*

CONTENTS

A CONTEXT FOR THIS BOOK

"The future will not be an extension of the past, but a new and different world entirely."

—DR. PETER DIAMANDIS, ENTREPRENEUR AND FUTURIST

Imagine waking up one morning to a world that feels like it's straight out of a science fiction novel. Your smartphone is no longer a device in your pocket, but a part of your very being. Industries that have been the backbone of our economy for decades, even generations, have been completely transformed by robots that can think, learn, and perform tasks with super-human precision. The entire world around you is filled with artificial intelligence, shaping the way you communicate, consume information, and experience the world.

Step outside, and you might see people immersed in virtual worlds, overlaid seamlessly onto the physical reality around them. In the sky above you see flying cars, or even catch a glimpse of one of the many spacecraft returning from Mars or from mining expeditions on distant asteroids, bearing precious metals that once seemed impossible to reach.

In this world, the boundaries of what's possible have been shattered. Surgeons have been outperformed by robotic precision, and the limits of human lifespan have been pushed back by decades. Entirely new industries have been born from the convergence of AI and quantum computing, while others have been swept away by the relentless tide of technological change.

Amid all this upheaval, there are new and exciting accomplishments. Entrepreneurs and innovators are harnessing these same technologies to tackle some of humanity's greatest challenges—clean water, access to education and opportunity, sustainable food production—and the solutions to these age-old problems are now within our grasp.

And perhaps most incredibly, this future isn't some distant fantasy. It's already unfolding before our eyes. Consider these technological realities that exist as of this book's writing:

- Right now, in Bangladesh, the World Bank is partnering with companies like Drinkwell to install water ATM booths that provide safe drinking water to thousands of people who previously had no access.
- Surgeons worldwide are being trained on Intuitive Surgical's da Vinci systems, which have already been used in more than 14 million robotic procedures.
- If you live in a rural area, you might already be one of the tens of millions of people globally who rely on satellite internet services, like Starlink, for reliable connectivity.
- You may have interacted with ChatGPT or another large language model (LLM) capable of understanding and generating human-like language, joining the hundreds of millions of users who engage with these systems every week.

- In a recent Mensa test, Open AI's LLM, o1, scored an IQ of 120, making it smarter than the average human.
- In some US cities you can already look up at the sky and spot a flying car—several models have already been approved by the US Federal Aviation Administration and are in commercial use.
- And in research labs like IBM's Thomas J. Watson Center, quantum computers are already solving in seconds problems that would take traditional supercomputers years, with the potential to revolutionize fields from climate science to drug discovery.

The future, in short, isn't some far-off destination. It's a journey that we're all on together, and it's happening faster than most of us can comprehend. The question is no longer whether these changes are coming, but how we'll adapt and thrive in a world that's changing more rapidly than ever before.

As you read these words, the world around us is transforming at a pace that's difficult to grasp. It's a rate of change that can leave us breathless, exhilarated, and perhaps a little bit terrified. On one hand, the possibilities of this new era are thrilling—a future of abundance, innovation, and exploration that our ancestors could scarcely have dreamed of. But on the other hand, the sheer scale and speed of this transformation raises a host of pressing questions:

- What will happen to you and your colleagues as your industry is reshaped by technological disruption? How will you adapt and continue to provide value?
- As entire new fields emerge, what kind of retraining and upskilling will you need to undertake to stay relevant and competitive?

- Which jobs and industries will fade into obsolescence, and what will become of the millions of workers who are displaced?
- How will the fabric of our cities change as remote work becomes the norm? What will happen to the bustling city centers that have been the heart of our economic life for centuries?
- As artificial intelligence grows more sophisticated, clearly surpassing human capabilities in most domains, what will be the impact on our work, our society, and our very identity as a species?
- In a world where more and more of our interactions happen in virtual spaces and across global distances, how will our fundamental need for human connection and community be reshaped?
- And as breakthroughs in medical science extend our lifespans by decades, how will we navigate this uncharted territory? How will we find meaning, purpose, and fulfillment in these bonus years?

These are questions that can keep us up at night, that can make us want to bury our heads in the sand and cling to the familiar comforts of the past. Many of us aren't even sure where to begin in terms of preparing for this uncertain future. What we do know is that the old rule book, the one that's guided us since the dawn of the industrial age, is being torn up before our eyes.

So how do we not just survive, but thrive, in the face of such transformative upheaval? The key, I believe, lies in our ability to adapt—and specifically, in our ability to harness and enhance our innate creative capability.

I'm not alone in this belief. NASA, an organization that

quite literally has its eyes fixed on the future, has launched a program specifically designed to identify and nurture its most creative engineers to lead the charge in solving tomorrow's challenges. The World Economic Forum, in its Future of Jobs Report, singles out innovation—which is simply creativity in action—as one of the most critical assets for any organization or economy navigating the turbulent waters ahead. And Linked-In Learning, in partnership with governments and NGOs around the world, has identified creativity as the number one "soft skill" that will be in demand globally, both now and for the foreseeable future.

This book aims to provide a pathway to developing our creative capability by strengthening the fundamental machinery of creativity within our own remarkable brain. The central argument of this book, what I call "The New Case for Creativity," is that musicianship–specifically, the process of learning to play a musical instrument—has a completely new role to play in preparing us for the rapidly unfolding future.

To fully grasp this connection, we'll need to explore the fundamental architecture of what makes us human, our deep innate relationship with music itself, and the specific ways that engaging in music reshapes our brain development and enhances creative capability.

WHO AM I TO BE WRITING A BOOK SUCH AS THIS?

Music has always been an integral part of who I am. From very early childhood onward, as I listened to and became familiar with any piece of music, I would begin to picture it in my mind's eye in terms of shapes and patterns. When I began studying piano at the age of seven, I would see those same shapes and patterns unfolding across the keyboard as my teacher played the songs I would be learning. This innate perspective of hearing music and seeing it through the lens of shapes and patterns formed the foundation of my entire musicianship.

As an adult, I made a profound discovery that would shape my life's work: I could explain my perspective of music in a way that allowed others to see it through the same lens as I do. In doing so, this transformed how quickly and easily people could learn to play music. Over the course of decades, I developed this perspective into a structured, scaffolded system of education, coupled with a comprehensive methodology for training educators. This became the Simply Music method, the cornerstone of the Simply Music organization, of which I am the founder.

Over the last several decades, I've had the privilege of personally training thousands of music educators from around the world and from diverse backgrounds. This includes those with advanced degrees and doctorates in music, classically trained pianists, symphony conductors, music therapists, music directors, jazz musicians, studio musicians, professional arrangers, composers, and performing artists. Equally important, I've trained music hobbyists, enthusiasts, self-taught novices, and relative beginners—many of whom had no idea they were capable of successfully teaching music. Through Simply Music, they have become accomplished educators maintaining thriving music-teaching studios.

The Simply Music method has enriched the lives of students across 136 countries, spanning all age groups from children to elders. We've also had decades of experience successfully teaching those navigating the complexities of special circumstances and learning differences, such as traumatic brain injuries, PTSD, blindness, deafness, Tourette's syndrome, profound autism, ADHD, and numerous other challenges.

My method has found its way into community centers,

private and public schools, and even penal institutions where I've personally taught incarcerated individuals in maximum-security prison.

As a published author and public speaker, I've shared my work through hundreds of presentations to audiences of all sizes, from intimate gatherings to groups of over a thousand. I am a TEDx speaker, an Oxford Talks presenter, and a speaker at the prestigious Gathering of Titans at MIT. My work has also been the subject of two independently written books.

I truly believe that my perspective is a gift and the result of divine design. As such, I don't claim to be the "creator" of my unique perspective. However, I recognize that my willingness to invest the tens of thousands of hours into bringing this gift to life has allowed me to build a wonderfully fulfilling life, contributing to the well-being of people worldwide. For this, I am deeply humbled and eternally grateful.

The key takeaways you can expect from this book include:

1. a deeper understanding of the technological changes reshaping our world and the imperative for developing creative capability.
2. insight into the neuroscience of how music learning enhances brain connectivity and supports creative capability.
3. a new perspective on the role of music education in preparing individuals and society for the challenges and opportunities of the future.

REVEALING MY PERSONAL BIAS

Before diving into the heart of this book, I must acknowledge the particular bias I bring to what I have to say. As an optimist,

I tend to see things positively, regardless of the struggles I've faced, believing I'm being prepared for something bigger and better.

Since 2012, I've had the privilege of being part of several entrepreneurial communities, surrounded by extraordinary people. It's exciting to be in rooms where I'm far from being the smartest person present. I've spent years in Joe Polish's Genius Network, Peter Diamandis's Abundance community, Giovanni Marsico's Archangel Academy, Steve Sims's Speakeasy community, and Dan Sullivan's Strategic Coach, where I regularly find myself on webinars with highly accomplished individuals discussing groundbreaking possibilities for humanity's benefit.

Peter Diamandis's Abundance community, in particular, has profoundly impacted me. At his events, I get firsthand experience of cutting-edge technologies that will transform the quality of life on Earth. I hear directly from scientists and researchers working on life extension and health-span expansion, discussing progress in extending healthy living to 120 years or beyond.

Initially, it was somewhat overwhelming trying to wrap my mind around these advancements, as most were far beyond my awareness. But over time, hearing again and again from world-leading experts speaking with certainty about developments that would elevate our collective quality of life, these possibilities have become normalized for me. I believe this is what's in store for humanity, and we're only a few years away from these technologies becoming more democratized and widely available.

I hold the same belief about the major global problems we face, such as starvation, illiteracy, lack of access to clean water, healthcare, education, and opportunity. Organizations and entrepreneurs are currently tackling all of these and more, committed to elevating humanity's quality of life.

It can be difficult to grasp this when our mainstream media bombards us primarily with what's going wrong in the world—the problems, crises, and fears, reported relentlessly. Yet, in the rooms I'm in, people are doing extraordinary things, making profound contributions worldwide. These accomplishments rarely get reported.

For so many years now I've been so immersed in positivity, optimism, and contribution to others that, quite simply, it's true for me. I also believe it supports humanity's well-being for more people to speak up about the wonderful era we're living in, the abundance of opportunities, and the immense goodness in the world.

I write this book through that lens—committed to being a voice that says if we can collectively see things positively, it contributes to that outcome becoming reality. I claim no ability to predict the future, but I know it's possible to create it, and we can all play a role.

With this understanding of my perspective, let's now dive into Part 1 of this book—exploring some of the extraordinary technological changes on the horizon, the crucial role of creativity in navigating this new landscape, and the transformative power of music learning in developing our creative capability. The stakes are high, but the path forward is clear—and it begins with harnessing the power of our own innate musicality.

PART 1

NAVIGATING THE TECHNOLOGICAL TIDAL WAVE

WHY CREATIVITY IS HUMANITY'S SUPERPOWER

Chapter 1

THE FUTURE IS JUST GETTING STARTED

"We cannot solve our problems with the same thinking we used when we created them."

—ALBERT EINSTEIN

Imagine this with me for a moment: 3D-printed housing communities within this very decade. Artificial Intelligence surpassing human cognitive skills by 2029. Nanorobots in our brains wirelessly connecting our cerebral cortex to the cloud by 2045.

When I first encountered these ideas, they sounded like science fiction to me too. But I now know that these advancements aren't just hypothetical—they're already in development, shaping our world in real time. The more I've learned, the more I've come to understand that the future we're racing toward isn't just a linear continuation of our past; we're accelerating up an exponential curve of technological advancement. As someone who has spent decades exploring human potential and creative expression, I couldn't help but wonder: What will this future demand of us? How can we cultivate the creativity and adaptability to not just survive, but thrive, in a world transformed?

When I talk about advancement, I'm not just referring to incrementally better laptops or smartphones—though it's worth noting that smartphones today can perform calculations 120 million times faster than the computers that took us to the moon. No, what I'm talking about is a technological tidal wave that's going to redefine life on Earth as we know it, that's going to transform the very essence of what it means to be human. It's nearly impossible to imagine any industry or arena that technology won't revolutionize, or make redundant—in other words, extinct. But at the same time, we'll see the emergence of entirely new industries, new opportunities, new possibilities that were unimaginable just decades ago.

As I contemplated this "new future," I found myself grappling with a profound realization: To thrive in this era of change, we will need to fundamentally rewire our thinking. The linear, sequential models that served us in the past will no longer suffice. Instead, we must cultivate a new way of seeing things, thinking about things, and doing things—in essence, a new way of being. This "new thinking" isn't about discarding our past, but about building on it, expanding our cognitive horizons to encompass the exponential shifts ahead. It's a daunting prospect, but also an exhilarating one—an invitation to step into the fullest expression of our potential.

THE EXPONENTIAL MIND SHIFT

If you join our 100 billion neurons with our 100 trillion connections, what you get is a human brain that determines everything we think and do. But here's the thing: Our brains evolved to function in the world we had over 100,000 years ago. It was a world that was very local, very linear, and very predictable.

Many of us remember a time when international communication meant writing letters that took weeks or months to arrive. Commerce and industry moved at an equally measured pace. Major changes unfolded over long periods, and linear thinking served us well.

But the world is now changing so significantly, and so rapidly, that the thinking of the past is no longer adequate for what's needed in this "current future" of exponential change. What we need now is exponential thinking—creative thinking.

When we describe something as "exponential," we're talking about a pattern of growth that continually accelerates, where each increase builds upon the previous ones, creating a growth curve that shoots upward dramatically rather than following a steady, straight-line progression. Think of it like this: If you fold a plain sheet of paper in half once, it becomes two layers thick; fold it again, it becomes four; another fold makes eight—each fold doubles the previous number, creating growth that becomes remarkably rapid. In the realm of technology, exponential advancement means that progress isn't just about adding small improvements year after year, but rather about each breakthrough building upon previous ones, leading to increasingly astounding leaps forward in shorter and shorter periods of time.

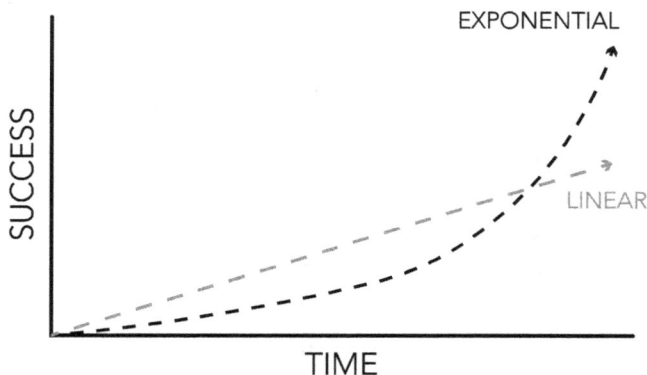

The fundamental difference between linear and exponential growth is stark: While they may look similar in the early stages, exponential change quickly becomes geometric. We now stand at the very "knee" of this exponential curve, and what that means is that the advancements we'll see in the next decade will dwarf everything that's happened in human history thus far.

Tomorrow's technologies—or rather, today's emerging technologies—aren't just redesigning our future. They're redefining how we must think about that future, and how we must think about ourselves within it. To flourish in this new world, humanity is going to have to become the most creative version of our species ever—what futurists are calling "Human 2.0."

THE LANGUAGE OF TOMORROW

When I first encountered terms like virtual reality, augmented reality, artificial intelligence, 3D printing, nanorobotics, NFTs, blockchain, cryptocurrency, life and healthspan extension, molecular repair and gene therapies, neural linking, brain–

computer interfacing, quantum computing—just to name a few—they seemed like something out of a sci-fi novel. But these are rapidly becoming part of our mainstream vocabulary. It's easy to feel overwhelmed by this onslaught of new concepts and capabilities. I know I certainly did. But as I grappled with these technologies and possibilities, I began to see a pattern—a world in which the boundaries of what's possible are expanding at an unprecedented rate. It's a world that both excites and humbles me, one that calls me to continually reexamine my assumptions about what the future might hold.

While we can't predict exactly how each of these technologies will develop, what we can do is observe how similar innovations have already transformed our world. Let's take a look at a few technologies that have achieved mass adoption and become seamlessly woven into the fabric of our daily lives, demonstrating the incredible speed at which new technologies can go from novelty to absolute necessity.

THE DIGITAL REVOLUTION: FROM INNOVATION TO NECESSITY

1. **The Internet**—Consider how quickly the internet became central to our very existence. When connectivity is disrupted even briefly, we experience it as a crisis—major industries falter, small businesses cease to function, our personal lives feel derailed. This transformation from novelty to necessity happened within a single generation.

2. **Personal Computing**—In the late 1980s, my first Compaq laptop was barely more portable than a carry-on suitcase, and had a mere 20 megabytes of hard drive space. Today, around 95 percent of US households own blazingly fast computers, with ownership reaching nearly 100 percent in

higher-income homes. The transition from luxury to utility is complete.

3. **Smartphones**—My first mobile phone in the early 1980s cost $5,000 and was roughly the size (and what seemed like the weight) of a brick. Today, nearly seven billion smartphones are in use globally. These devices have absorbed and replaced the functionality of cameras, GPS devices, typewriters, alarm clocks, calculators, televisions, flashlights, music players, and countless other tools—all in a pocket-sized device that's fundamentally changed how we interact with the world.

4. **Digital Transactions**—Since PayPal's emergence in the early 2000s, digital payment systems have revolutionized commerce. The market, currently exceeding $102 billion, is projected to reach $500 billion in the coming years. The sight of people paying for coffee with smartphones or smartwatches has become commonplace.

5. **Transportation Evolution**—What began with two friends' frustration over trying to find a taxi late at night in Paris became Uber, birthing a $50 billion global rideshare industry expected to double by 2030. This transformation goes beyond convenience—it's reshaping vehicle ownership, urban planning, and our relationship with transportation itself.

6. **Accommodation Revolution**—Airbnb's journey, from two friends sharing an air mattress at another friend's apartment in San Francisco to a $117 billion company surpassing the combined market value of Marriott, Hyatt, and Hilton, exemplifies how quickly new models can disrupt established industries.

7. **Retail Transformation**—Amazon's evolution from an online bookstore to a $2 trillion market force demonstrates

how technology can fundamentally alter consumer behavior. E-commerce has become so ingrained that we're surprised and frustrated when we can't instantly order what we need with next-day, or even same-day, delivery!

THE HORIZON: TEN TRANSFORMATIVE TECHNOLOGIES

While these past innovations are impressive, they represent only the beginning. Let's now explore a few (of a multitude of) transformational technologies that are poised to reshape our world and demand unprecedented levels of human creativity and adaptability.

1. **Global Connectivity**—By 2030, over 90 percent of humanity—more than 7.5 billion people—will be connected online. This isn't just about communication; it represents billions of minds joining the global economy, accessing education, and contributing their creativity to solving world problems. The Internet itself, and our access to it, is also being transformed. As Susan Etlinger of the Altimeter Group notes, "What we know as our internet will be largely obsolete. Our digital interactions will be conversational, haptic, and embedded in the world we live in—even, to some extent, in ourselves."

2. **Solar Energy**—Every hour, more solar energy reaches Earth than humanity uses in a year. While we're still developing efficient capture methods, renewable energy initiatives led by China, the USA, and Japan are revolutionizing how we power our world. Imagine the creative possibilities when clean, sustainable energy becomes universally available.

3. **Clean Water Access**—With over a quarter of the world's population lacking access to clean water—resulting in 3.5 million deaths annually—creative solutions are emerging:

A. Fog harvesting in Morocco generating thousands of daily liters

B. Solar-powered filtration systems producing 20,000 daily liters

C. Israeli desalination technology—turning ocean water into drinking water—serving forty countries. These innovations demonstrate how creative thinking can solve humanity's most pressing challenges.

4. **Cultured Food Production**—While nine million people die annually from hunger, creative biotechnology solutions are emerging. Lab-grown meat requires 90 percent less water and land than traditional farming, with a near-zero carbon footprint. This technology could end global hunger while dramatically reducing environmental impact—a testament to human creativity solving multiple problems simultaneously.

5. **Vertical Farming**—Agriculture's first major revolution since 10,000 BC is underway. Vertical farming exemplifies creative problem-solving: producing more food with less space, water, and environmental impact. This transformative agricultural technology grows crops in stacked layers inside controlled indoor environments. It allows fresh produce to be grown year-round in urban areas, even in previously unsuitable locations like abandoned warehouses or underground spaces.

6. **Transportation Revolution**—Autonomous vehicles and eVTOLs (electric vertical takeoff and landing aircraft—think "flying cars") aren't just about convenience—they're about reimagining human mobility. These technologies, already in use and being commercialized, could eliminate the 1.3 million annual traffic deaths while transforming urban planning and introducing an entirely unprecedented level of cleanness, quietness, and safety.

7. **Advanced Manufacturing**—3D and 4D printing are revolutionizing how we create everything. These technologies "print" three-dimensional objects by depositing materials, layer by layer, allowing for the creation of complex shapes and structures. This technology is already transforming various industries, from manufacturing and medicine to construction and aerospace, providing the ability to print everything from buildings to human organs.

8. **Robotics and Cobotics**—Beyond replacing dangerous jobs, robots are becoming collaborative partners—"cobots"—in creative problem-solving. They can perform precise surgical procedures and provide elder care support and companionship. AI-powered domestic robots combine artificial intelligence, sensors, and sophisticated mechanics to perform household tasks autonomously. They're capable of cooking, cleaning, laundry folding, and even providing basic caregiving support, all while understanding verbal commands, recognizing family members, and navigating homes safely.

9. **Space Exploration**—The quest to become a multiplanetary species isn't just about survival—it's about expanding human creativity beyond Earth's boundaries. As Elon Musk notes, it's about "the expansion and extension of the scope and scale of consciousness." Previous space innovations gave us everything from camera phones, CAT scans, and water purifiers to wireless headsets, artificial limbs, and memory foam. Imagine what creative solutions Mars colonization might spawn that will have significant, far-reaching, and positive impact here on planet Home.

10. **Lifespan Extension**—Harvard University's Dr. David Sinclair is approaching aging as a "software problem" with solutions. He states, "The discovery that aging is controlled

by our genes and can be reversed gives us more years of health, not just more years of life. This is no longer a question of if, but when."[1] Futurist Ray Kurzweil, with his 86 percent accuracy rate in predictions, suggests we'll reach "Longevity Escape Velocity" by 2030—where each year lived adds more than a year to life expectancy.[2] This extension of human lifespan will require unprecedented creativity in reimagining careers, relationships, and purpose.

THE CREATIVE IMPERATIVE

These technologies are converging to create an entirely new reality. As we face questions about AI decision-making, 120-plus-yearlong healthspans, and human–technology integration, one thing becomes crystal clear: Our survival and our ability to thrive will depend on our creative capability.

The decade ahead will introduce more change than all of human history combined. Through nanotechnology, augmented reality, and brain–computer interfaces, we'll witness the emergence of humanity becoming more and more a hybrid biological/nonbiological species. Our smartphones already analyze our behavior patterns; soon, nanorobots will monitor our blood chemistry while AI manages our nutrition through smart fridges and drone deliveries.

When I first grasped the scale and speed of these technological advancements, I felt a mixture of awe and apprehension. It's one thing to imagine these scenarios in the abstract; it's quite another to realize they're already unfolding, shaping our world in real time. As I contemplated the implications, I found

---

1   Abundance360, event, March 21, 2023, Palos Verdes, California.

2   Ray Kurzweil, "Metaverse," webinar, attended by author, February 3, 2022.

myself grappling with a profound question: How can we, as individuals and as a society, cultivate the creative capacity to not just weather these changes, but to harness them for the greater good? It's a question I continue to wrestle with, and one I invite you to explore with me throughout this book.

A PATH FORWARD—MUSIC

We must reconcile with technology's role not as a replacement for human connection, but as an extension of human capability. Just as the industrial revolution amplified our physical abilities, this technological revolution is amplifying our creative and intellectual abilities.

The main thing to understand here is that life, as we know it, is about to be drastically different. And if we are to thrive and flourish in this new future, it will demand that we learn how to look at our lives, and ourselves, through an entirely new lens. While so much of this can seem unpredictable, one certainty is that humanity needs to become the most creative version of our species, ever—Human 2.0—described by Professor Hugh Herr of the MIT Media Lab as "an era where technology will merge with our bodies and our minds to forever change our concept of human capability."[3]

And remarkably, we have access to a powerful tool for enhancing creativity that we discovered over 60,000 years ago: music. The Divje Babe flute, crafted from a cave bear's thigh bone, represents humanity's earliest known musical instrument.

---

[3] "The New Era of Human 2.0: New Minds, New Bodies, New Identities," event description, MIT Media Lab Events, Princeton University, accessed January 15, 2025, https://www.media.mit.edu/events/new-era-human-20-new-minds-new-bodies-new-identities/.

Recent research suggests music preceded language, providing the foundation for human creative expression.

As we'll discover, musicality isn't a gift for the chosen few—it's a fundamental and profoundly human capability waiting to be awakened. And to this, some will question, "What? Learning music? But what if I'm not musical?"

These are questions I've heard many times over. And before we can dive into gaining a deeper understanding of the role that musicianship can play in developing our creative capability, we must address these questions. They're actually an obstacle that's in our way, and have prevented a great many people, over a very long time, from reaping the benefits that music has to offer. In the next chapter, let's tackle these questions head-on and remove that obstacle once and for all.

Chapter 2

WE ARE A MUSICAL SPECIES

.

"Everything you can imagine is real. Every child is an artist. The problem is how to remain an artist once we grow up."

—PABLO PICASSO

WHAT IF I'M NOT MUSICAL?

Let me ask you a question: Have you ever found yourself saying, or thinking, "I'm just not musical"? If so, you're far from alone. At every presentation I give, I ask three simple questions of my audience. First: "Who here believes they're a 'musical person'?" A few hesitant hands rise. Second: "Who isn't sure?" More hands go up. Finally: "Who believes they're not musical?" Almost invariably, the majority of hands are raised.

This scene repeats itself in different forms everywhere I go. During rideshare trips, upon learning I'm a music educator, drivers often speak similarly: "I love music, but I've got no music in me," or "I couldn't hold a tune if you paid me," or "I tried music lessons as a kid, but had no talent." These responses reveal a deeply entrenched, multicultural paradigm—an unquestioned belief that musicality is a gift bestowed upon only a select few.

In my decades of teaching and sharing music, I've encountered this belief countless times—the notion that some people are simply "not musical." And each time, it breaks my heart a little. Because here's the truth—the realization that has shaped my life's work: **Every single human being, without exception, is deeply, profoundly musical.** It's not a gift bestowed on a chosen few; it's an inherent part of our human design. In fact, we're so fundamentally musical that we often don't even notice it, like a fish swimming in water. This book is my attempt to shine a light on that water, to invite you to see and experience the musicality that's always been within you. Together, I believe we can democratize musicality, expand its definition, and recognize that being human and being musical are one and the same.

THE OBVIOUS HIDDEN IN PLAIN SIGHT

There's a fine line between oblivious and obvious. Sometimes we can't see the forest for the trees—our innate musicality hides in plain sight. Let me show you what I mean through everyday examples that surround us.

Picture this: We're walking down the street, deep in conversation. Our focus is entirely on our dialogue, yet underlying our actions is an unconscious rhythm: left, right, left, right, left, right. We're not thinking about walking—there's no effort, no theory, no mathematics involved. What's happening in the background is a perfectly smooth, natural, and beautifully even musical rhythm. That, my friend, is profound musicality!

Now, consider these common scenarios:

You arrive at a location and knock on the door:

Knock… Knock… Knock… Knock… Knock.

Try it now on your lap or table. Notice the natural, effortless rhythm that emerges.

You slice a loaf of bread, the knife moving back and forth:

Crsh… Crsh… Crsh… Crsh… Crsh.

Listen closely to the beautiful, unconscious rhythm.

Construction workers in a nearby house drive nails into a wall:

Bang… Bang… Bang… Bang… Bang.

A different intensity but the same underlying musicality.

You brush your teeth before bed:

Shh… Shh… Shh… Shh… Shh… Shh.

Another perfect, natural rhythm.

If I spent just one morning with you, I could point out dozens of instances where you unconsciously demonstrate mastery over your innate musicality. I encourage you to start noticing these moments. Make it a conscious practice to listen for the musicality that you express, and that surrounds you every hour of every day. The complex musicality that underscores human existence is undeniable once you begin to notice it. Practice becoming conscious of it.

Consciousness creates connection, not only at an emotional and psychological level, but also at a neurological level, and creative capability has everything to do with neural connectivity.

THE MUSIC IN OUR WORDS

Perhaps the most powerful example lies in our speech itself. I couldn't possibly count the number of times that people have said to me, "I haven't got a musical bone in my body."

I respond to this by asking them to listen to what they just said—not to the words themselves, but to the rhythm of the syllables:

"I haven't got a musical bone in my body."

"I haven't got a musical bone in my body."

"I haven't got a musical bone in my body."

Within this simple sentence lives an incredibly complex rhythmical pattern: "a-rat-a-tat-a-tat-a-tat-taaaa...rat-a-tat-a"

This sophisticated rhythmicality underscores the syllables. While this example may seem abstract in written words, the musicality of speech becomes clear when we analyze its components: the complexity of rhythm, variations in emphasis, dynamics of pitch, shifts in expression, and modulations of tone. Our spoken language demonstrates an extraordinary mastery over astonishingly complex musical concepts.

(Note: For a clear demonstration of this concept, you can watch my TEDx Talk on YouTube, "How Music Can Future-Proof Your Brain," where I guide an entire audience to connect to the intricate musicality of language.)

FACT: We can't utter a single sentence without demonstrating mastery over complex musical concepts.

It's our musicality that gave birth to language in the first place. We're a music-making species—it's fundamental to human nature. Our heartbeat, breath, actions, and language all testify to this truth: To be human is to be musical.

FROM OBLIVIOUS TO OBVIOUS

Humanity has always responded to rhythmic and tonal vibrations—in nature's sounds, religious rituals, and our earliest conversations. We're physiological beings, psychological beings, and for many, spiritual beings. No culture in human history has existed without looking beyond itself to some form of higher power. Similarly, I assert that we're musical beings, functioning moment by moment, and unconsciously expressing extraordinarily complex musicality.

Why is it so essential for us to recognize this? Because in truly understanding how profoundly musical we are, it validates all of us being able to explore musicianship as a unique and powerful means of developing our creative capability—a crucial skill for flourishing in our rapidly evolving future.

But how we can help people connect with and develop their natural musicianship in a way that aligns with brain design, and remains accessible to everyone. This requires redefining "musicality" itself. The common perception—that being musical means excelling at playing an instrument, singing, or dancing—is far too narrow, too limiting, and fundamentally inaccurate.

We need a broader understanding and definition of musicality, one that reflects our true nature as humans. When I speak of us being a musical species, I'm referring to the rhythmicity that underscores all our gestures and functionality. Even at the quantum level we're composed of subatomic strings that are vibrating us into existence.

LOOKING FORWARD

If we are to flourish in our technologically advanced future, and to harness these innovations to enhance our lives, we must expand our thinking. Why? Because amid all the emerging technologies and transformations, one critical personal attribute will dominate the future: creativity.

Let's recap our journey so far. We've examined:

- Technology's profound impact on our world.

- The pipeline of innovations poised to redefine human existence.
- How these technologies' convergence will transform our world at breathtaking speed.
- The need to rethink our identity as a species.
- The unpredictability of our future.
- The imperative for humanity to emerge as its most creative version ever—Human 2.0.

We've also discovered:

- The challenge this presents to those who believe they're "not musical."
- The universal, profound musicality present in all humans.
- How this musicality manifests in our daily actions and interactions.
- The potential for musical development to enhance creative capability.

As we move forward, and just as we've unveiled our inherent musicality, we'll also discover that we're also inherently creative beings. Understanding this connection is key to unlocking our potential in a rapidly evolving world. But what exactly is creativity? Let's explore this crucial question in our next chapter.

Chapter 3

THE NEW CASE
FOR CREATIVITY

"The Theory of Relativity occurred to me by intuition, and music is the driving force behind that intuition. My new discovery is the result of musical perception."

—ALBERT EINSTEIN

REDEFINING CREATIVITY

In the previous chapter, we touched on how when people think of someone as being "musical," they most commonly think of someone who's competent at playing an instrument, singing, or dancing. A similar thing occurs when people describe someone as being "creative." We often picture someone with an unusual fashion sense, an artistic career, or an unconventional lifestyle. Further to this, in our modern world with its emphasis on industry, economics, and systems, creativity has been relegated to the sidelines—viewed as a playful but nonessential pursuit.

Creative careers are often dismissed as impractical "side gigs" rather than viable professions.

As someone who's dedicated my life to fostering creative expression, I've often found myself frustrated by the way our educational systems marginalize the creative arts. It's a trend I've observed with concern, even as I've been heartened by voices like Daniel Pink, whose 2005 book, *A Whole New Mind*, argued persuasively for the rising importance of right-brain, creative thinking. Yet despite this recognition, I still see a pervasive undervaluing of creativity in our societal priorities and structures. It's a blind spot that I believe we must address if we're to fully harness our creative potential in the face of the challenges ahead.

Just as we need to redefine musicality, I believe we also need a more practical and democratized definition of creativity. We need a definition that's both simple and relatable—one that helps reprioritize creativity's role in our lives and broadens access to its development.

DEMOCRATIZING CREATIVITY

The subject of creativity has filled countless books, and scientific exploration reveals that the neurology of creativity is vast and complex. There's also a commonly agreed upon description of creativity as the process of creating something unique that's brought into the world and is generally considered to have value. I'm of the view that the emphasis on "value" is problematic.

Consider Vincent van Gogh, who died in 1890. Throughout his lifetime, he lived in poverty and sold only one painting for 400 francs. Yet a full century later, his *Portrait of Dr. Gachet* commanded $82.5 million ($190 million by today's value). If we judge creativity by contemporary value, we must conclude that van Gogh wasn't creative during his lifetime but became creative a century after his death—an obvious absurdity. Clearly, the "perceived value" component of traditional creativity definitions needs reconsidering.

Let's democratize creativity with a more practical definition. At its core, creativity is about:

- seeing things differently.
- thinking about things differently.
- doing things differently.

Consider the following:

- Our ability to see an opportunity where others may not—that is a direct function of creativity.
- Our ability to materialize that perceived opportunity and to assemble whatever is needed to make it happen—that is a direct function of creativity.
- Our ability to resolve the problems and challenges that arise along the way—that is a direct function of creativity.

So, if seeing opportunities in life, implementing opportunities in life, and problem-solving in life are all a function of creativity—if it's that important (which it is!)—then, **what activity are we consciously weaving into the fabric of our lives that's specifically designed to neurologically develop our creative capability?**

Musicianship—specifically, learning to play music—does this in a most unique and wonderful way.

"CREATIVE CAPABILITY" AS DISTINCT
FROM "CREATIVE EXPRESSION"

Here we should clarify that there is an important distinction between "creative capability" and "creativity" itself. Creative capability is the neurological component—the machinery that enables creativity—in thinking and action. Creativity (which, more accurately is "creative expression") is the output of creative capability—what we actually create.

Think of it this way, and let's use physical performance as an analogy: If Olympic sprinter Usain Bolt and I walk down the street at the same pace, our "performance expression" is identical, but his "performance capability" far exceeds mine. Similarly, if I drive a vintage Volkswagen Beetle alongside a new Porsche 911, and both cars are proceeding at twenty-five miles per hour, our "performance expression" matches, but the Porsche's "performance capability" is vastly greater.

This distinction matters because our ability to thrive in the future depends not just on creative expression, but even more so on developing our brain's creative capability—the neural machinery that determines how easily, effectively, and to what extent we can think and act creatively.

NEURAL CONNECTIVITY: THE FOUNDATION
OF CREATIVE CAPABILITY

A central argument of this book is that neural connectivity directly correlates with creative capability. Simply put: A more neurally connected brain is a more creatively capable brain.

Think of it like a road system. Imagine you need to travel from point A to point B, and there are four direct roads connecting the two points. You have four options to choose from.

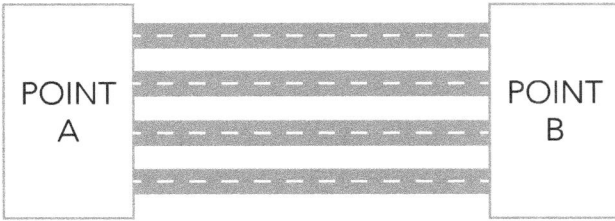

Now, add just one more road that connects these four existing routes, and suddenly your options expand from four to sixteen possible paths.

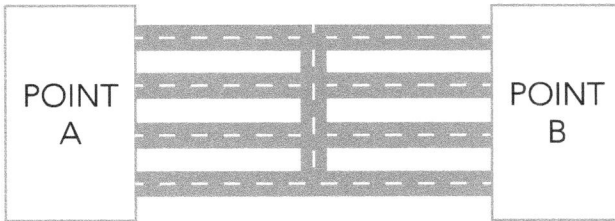

This simple analogy illustrates how increased connectivity multiplies possibilities—the essence of creative thinking.

DEMOCRATIZING THE VISIONARY

As I've explored the nature of creativity, I've come to realize that our concept of what it means to be a "visionary" is in need of a similar democratization. Too often, we reserve this term for the rare individuals whose achievements reshape industries or even society as a whole—the Elon Musks and Steve Jobses of the world, the visionaries whose names become synonymous with innovation on a grand scale. But the more I've contemplated the essence of visionary thinking, the more I've come to believe that it's not the exclusive domain of a select few. Rather, it's a fundamental human capacity, one we all possess, even if we don't always recognize it in ourselves. This realization has been both humbling and empowering for me, a reminder that the potential for visionary impact lies within each of us—**all human beings are naturally visionary beings.**

Consider these examples:

- Two children imagine building a tree house, carefully planning each step. They gather some wood and rope, borrow hammers and nails, and work on it after school and on weekends until it's built.
- A couple imagines creating a nursery for their expected child. They carefully plan and design the layout, get the necessary permits, hire contractors where needed, and complete adding the extension to their existing home.
- An entrepreneur imagines a multiplanetary future for humanity. He assembles a global team of experts to assist him. He gets governmental approval and support, raises the financial resources needed, creates breakthrough technologies, and builds a new generation of rockets to make it happen.

The only difference between these three examples? Scale. The five fundamental components of the visionary process remain identical:

1. Clearly envisioning a possibility
2. Articulating and enrolling others in the vision
3. Empowering others to act toward its fulfillment
4. Assembling the necessary resources
5. Having an unstoppable commitment through to completion

Whether building a tree house or colonizing Mars, these five elements remain constant. This reveals an important truth: Being visionary isn't reserved for a select few—it's fundamental to human nature, a fundamental recognition of human capability. Every time someone solves a novel problem, imagines a better way, or brings a new idea to life, they're demonstrating creativity and being a visionary—in both thinking and action.

CREATIVITY IN ACTION

Creativity isn't just about groundbreaking inventions or artistic masterpieces—it's alive in the everyday moments of human ingenuity. Consider nine-year-old Lily Hooks, who watched her sister scraping candle wax, while her father struggled applying adhesive to a torn mesh window screen. Lily had an insight: Why not use wax as an adhesive? In that moment, something clicked—a connection between two seemingly unrelated events that led to an $18 million innovation. As Steve Jobs perfectly captured it, "Creativity is just connecting things."

This simple truth plays out all around us, in ways both small and profound. Look into any home, school, or workplace, and you'll find creativity flourishing. It's in the ten-year-old who rigs a clever pulley system to deliver snacks to their tree house, the teenager who develops an emoji-based note-taking system, or the child who transforms room cleaning into an engaging game. These aren't just cute stories—they're clear examples of our innate creative capability at work.

The workplace becomes a laboratory for creative thinking when we look closely. Every day, people are finding innovative ways to solve problems and improve processes. A receptionist develops a filing system that saves hours of work. A warehouse worker discovers a more efficient storage pattern. A nurse creates a better method for tracking patient medications. Each of these represents creativity in action—not the kind that makes headlines, but the kind that makes life better.

The global pandemic showed us something crucial about human nature: Faced with unprecedented challenges and needing to be fully self-reliant, our innate creativity emerged powerfully. People who lost businesses or jobs didn't just survive—they innovated, finding solutions to problems they never imagined facing. This worldwide demonstration of adaptability wasn't exceptional—it revealed our natural creative and visionary capabilities. Neighbors created rotating childcare systems. Local businesses developed innovative, contactless delivery methods. Communities transformed unused lots into thriving gardens.

Each solution arose from the same creative process that drives world-changing innovations—the only difference was scale. And here I want to point out what I call the "scale illusion"—the misconception that there's a fundamental difference between everyday creativity and world-changing innovation. Consider how Uber essentially scaled up the concept of a neighborhood carpool system, or how Instagram grew from the same human desire that drives us to share photo albums at family gatherings. PayPal? At its core, it's a digitized version of the same principles that govern a local barter system.

We're standing at a crucial turning point in human history. Ray Kurzweil's prediction that "The next decade will see artificial intelligence master every human skill, one after another" isn't science fiction—it's unfolding before our eyes.[4] Think about the skilled accountant whose routine tasks are being automated, the radiologist whose diagnostic work is being matched or exceeded by AI, or the truck driver facing the reality of autonomous vehicles. These aren't distant possibilities—they're current challenges, they're happening now, and they're requiring creative solutions.

As AI and automation master routine tasks, our value as humans will increasingly lie in our creative capabilities. This isn't just about artistic expression—it's about creative problem-solving, adaptive thinking, and vision implementation. We need to be able to identify unprecedented challenges, develop novel solutions, and connect unexpected dots. We must learn to navigate uncertainty, find opportunities in chaos, and reimagine possibilities.

A NASA study found that 98 percent of four- and five-year-olds scored at "creative genius" level. By age ten, only 30 percent maintained this level, and by age fifteen, just 12 percent. Among adults, merely 2 percent reached this threshold. This decline isn't inevitable—it's the result of environmental factors. Our current approach to education contributes significantly to separating us from expressing our creativity. Studies show that only 22 percent of creative capability comes from genetics; the remaining 78 percent stems from nurture. No one is born uncreative. We are all born creative, and our creative capability can either grow or diminish based on how we nurture it.[5]

4   Abundance360, event, March 20, 2024, Palos Verdes, California.

5   George Land, "TEDxTucson George Land the Failure of Success," TEDx Talks, February 11, 2016, YouTube video, 13:06, https://www.youtube.com/watch?v=ZfKMq-rYtnc.

THE MUSICAL BRIDGE TO OUR CREATIVE FUTURE

We're entering an era of potential abundance, with technologies promising universal clean energy, abundant clean water, sustainable food production, and extended lifespans. But this creates new challenges: finding purpose beyond survival, creating meaning in a post-scarcity world, and developing new forms of contribution. These challenges require that we see things differently, think about things differently, and do things differently.

Consider the implications of extended lifespans. If longevity research succeeds in extending healthy lifespans to 120 years or beyond, how will you spend those additional decades? What will you create when financial survival isn't your primary concern? Will you have friends, community, a sense of belonging? How will you contribute to a world of abundance?

This is where music enters the picture in a surprising and powerful way. Think of music as a gym for creative capability. Musicianship develops the same fundamental capabilities required by an entrepreneur adapting to market changes, a parent solving a family crisis, or a community addressing new challenges. These capabilities—pattern recognition, real-time adaptation, creative problem-solving, collaborative thinking, and innovative implementation—are universal tools for navigating an uncertain future.

THE CREATIVITY AND VISIONARY PARTNERSHIP

And now we stand at a pivotal moment in human history. The approaching technological tsunami will redefine not just how we live, but what it means to be human. As artificial intelligence and revolutionary technologies transform or eliminate centuries-old industries, we must develop our creative capability as a means of enabling us to navigate this disruption. This isn't just about learning new skills—it's about becoming conscious of, awakening, and developing what's already within us.

For too long, we've mystified creativity and vision, treating them as rare gifts rather than natural human traits. The truth is simpler: Creativity means seeing, thinking about, and doing things differently. Being visionary means imagining possibilities and bringing them into reality. These aren't magical abilities—they're fundamental aspects of being human that we must now consciously develop.

Part of the key lies in understanding how our brains grow. When we engage in creative activities, particularly learning and playing music, we exponentially increase neural connectivity. This enhanced connectivity directly improves our creative capability, and this directly impacts our ability to adapt, innovate, and thrive.

The future isn't about competing with artificial intelligence or resisting technological change—it's about developing our uniquely human capabilities to shape these changes thoughtfully and ethically. While some may resist change, agility will become a fundamental requirement. As Peter Diamandis notes, "The best way to predict the future is to create it yourself."

The future belongs to those who develop these inherent capabilities. This isn't optional—it's essential for flourishing in the world we're entering. We must embrace this development not from fear, but from recognition of our extraordinary human potential. Our and our children's ability to thrive depends on the actions we take today.

THE PATH FORWARD

So, precisely what does it mean to take action? Well, let's break it down. We now know that technologies are coming down the pipeline that will not only redefine our world but will redefine what it means to be human. As a means of not merely functioning, but flourishing in this new future, we're going to need to see things differently, think about things differently, and do things differently. In other words, we're going to need enhanced creativity as a vital personal attribute. If we're to develop and enhance our creativity, then we need to impact the machinery that determines our creative capability, and how we achieve that is by doing anything and everything we can that directly impacts neural connectivity. In other words, we need to nourish and grow our brains.

And it's right here where music enters the picture. Remember that Divje Babe flute from 60,000 years ago? It's not just an artifact—it's evidence of humanity's innate connection to creative expression through music. We were playing music before we even had language!

In my years of teaching and advocating for music education, I've witnessed firsthand the transformative power of learning to play an instrument. But it's what we're learning now about the neuroscience of music that's helped me to understand just how profound that transformation can be. I've now come to see that musicianship—specifically, learning to play—provides a unique form of "neurological nutrition"—a way of nourishing and growing the brain, enhancing neural connectivity, and developing the creative capability that will be so essential in navigating the future. It's a realization that's filled me with a renewed sense of purpose and urgency in my work. Because in a very real sense, when we engage in music learning, we're not just enriching our present—we're investing in our future cognitive health and creative potential.

Who would've thought that in this era of extraordinary technological advancements, one of the most remarkable support tools that could help us live powerfully and effectively in this new future was to reconnect with something so uniquely and innately human—the ability to play music? Remember: Creativity isn't a gift given to a chosen few—it's a fundamental human capability waiting to be developed.

In the next chapter, let's explore the multitude of unique and extraordinary ways in which musicianship does this.

Chapter 4

MUSIC AS CRITICAL NEUROLOGICAL NUTRITION

"If we could harness the creativity of the brain and make people ten percent more creative in this world, I think we could change civilization."

—DR. CHARLES LIMB

Music, in both its role and value, is fundamental to every culture on Earth. As we discussed earlier, we can see evidence of its origins dating back to our Neanderthal relatives of 60,000 years ago. Clearly there are significant differences, from one culture to the next, in what form music takes, but its presence and importance is indisputable. In some cultures, music is so intrinsically woven into the fabric of that culture that there is largely no distinction between music, talking, and dancing.

The evolving level of consciousness of cultures is reflected in the ever-changing genres and styles of music that emerge from one generation to the next. Our history is reflected in music; our stories are told with music. We celebrate our major victories with music. We share in the mourning of the loss of loved ones with music. Our deepest memories of wonderful times, and tragic times, are commonly intimately connected with the music that we played during those times. It's fundamental to every rite of passage. We dance to music; we study to music; it's the background to an intimate dinner; it powerfully creates the ebb and flow of our emotions as it quietly underscores the movie or TV show we're watching. It's our battle song, our love song, our victory song, our worship music, our meditation score, and our therapist.

In essence, in its simplest and purest form, human beings love music. We value music, we need music and, no matter what, it's here to stay—it's who we are as a profoundly musical species.

THE SCIENCE OF MUSIC AND CREATIVE CAPABILITY

As I've immersed myself in the study of music's impact on the brain, I've been struck again and again by the depth and breadth of its influence. The more I learn, the more I'm convinced that the neurological benefits of music learning have implications that extend far beyond the realm of music itself. This realization has been both exhilarating and sobering for me. Exhilarating because it suggests that music may hold a key to unlocking human potential in ways we're only beginning to understand. Sobering because it underscores the urgency of ensuring that music learning is accessible to all, not just to a privileged few. As we stand on the threshold of a new era, one in which the challenges we face will demand an unprecedented level of creativity and adaptability, I can't help but wonder: What role might music play in equipping us to meet those challenges head-on? It's a question that's come to drive my work and my passion.

Science is on our side. For decades now, scientists have continued to learn and reveal more and more about the value of musicianship—the impact that music has on our bodies, our minds, our psychology, our emotions and our intelligence. We have a clear understanding of the fact that music is a powerful force that has a great deal to contribute to our wholeness as humans, our capabilities, and our general well-being.

Ironically, in spite of several hundred years of formal music education, and in spite of the populations of people who have struggled and failed at learning music, it's still widely regarded as being important and highly desirable. Yet for all that we've learned, modern cultures continue to regard music as a pleasant activity, a nice hobby, a valuable and good thing, but still generally not as important as studies in the area of science, technology, engineering, and math.

But this needs to change. Our regard for music, the value we place on it, and the role that it has to play in modern society need to adapt to meet the demands and complexities of the extraordinary new future that humanity is about to face.

Current research, while still in its infancy, is giving us a new understanding of the enormous benefits that musicianship has to offer.[6] But of even greater importance is to recognize that our ability to see, think, and act differently; our ability to exercise agility; our ability to change and grow are governed by our creative capability. And creative capability, as I've stated previously in this book, has everything to do with neural connectivity. **A more connected brain is a more creatively capable brain.**

---

6   Music News, ScienceDaily, accessed January 15, 2025, https://www.sciencedaily.com/news/mind_brain/music/.

Dr. Charles Limb, a leading neuroscientist in the study of music and brain activity, believes that creative musicianship makes a distinctive contribution to the brain's expansion. When considering this, he states, "Improvisation as a prototype that is creative involves a different neural signature than rote, or memorized, playing. To me, this is a profound statement. Because it does suggest that the value of creativity may be more evolutionary and life sustaining than something that's in the realm of entertainment or enjoyment. And I think that is critical."[7]

Even so, Dr. Limb cautions us. He states, "Our discoveries in this area are staggering, but relatively new. This is a field that's in its infancy."[8] As such, from the scientific perspective, we must be cautious in interpreting this evidence as proven fact. Limb does, however, go so far as to give a nod to a high probability of validity. As he puts it, "There are a lot of levels of evidence that suggest there are a whole host of traits, or characteristics, that are brought out or encouraged or promoted in the brain by something like musical training or musical improvisation. Let's call it neural flexibility. I think all of those things are supported by musical networks that are forcing the brain to do these kinds of mental gymnastics. Why shouldn't there be a transference of that to other more holistic types of things that affect your life?"

CAN MUSIC BE TO THE BRAIN WHAT EXERCISE IS TO THE BODY?

What if learning to play music could do for your brain what physical exercise does for your body? Imagine the impact: Just as running, weight lifting, or practicing yoga builds muscle,

---

7 Dr. Charles Limb, interview by author, April 26, 2023.

8 Limb, interview by author.

flexibility, and endurance, music learning acts like a mental gym, activating a full range of cognitive functions. The analogy is simple, but the concept is profound. Music learning isn't just an activity; it's a comprehensive workout for the brain. In the same way that exercise builds physical resilience, learning music builds cognitive resilience.

One study using representative data from the German Socio-Economic Panel (SOEP) found that learning music impacts both cognitive and noncognitive skills more than twice as much as sports and other forms of art.[9] What an extraordinary thing to consider!

As science dives deeper into the effects of musical training, we see that music learning engages the brain in three primary and powerful ways:

- It provides vast, multiregional brain engagement, where auditory, motor, and executive functions work in sync.
- It expands the brain's neural connectivity and creates the pathways essential for cognitive health.
- It enhances connectivity-driven creative capability— boosting the brain's capacity to connect ideas, form novel associations, and engage in complex, creative problem-solving.

It's crucial to clarify, though, that these benefits are unique to actively learning music—not simply listening to it. When we listen to music, we clearly experience a powerful but passive stimulation of auditory and emotional centers, but it's through

---

9   Adrian Hille and Jürgen Schupp, "How Learning a Musical Instrument Affects the Development of Skills," discussion paper no. 7655, IZA, September 2013, https://docs.iza.org/dp7655.pdf.

learning and playing music that the brain forms far more powerful and enduring connections.

Let's explore a simple summary of just some of the benefits that musicianship has on the brain. We'll consider these through the lens of how music learning can possibly serve as the brain's answer to modern challenges. We'll discover that, much like training in a gym builds a healthy body, music training cultivates a healthy mind and a creative brain, primed to adapt to an ever-changing world.

THE NEURAL SYMPHONY: HOW MUSIC TRANSFORMS OUR BRAIN

Music, as any musician will tell you, isn't simply "played." It's orchestrated—mentally and physically—tapping into the mind's full array of functions. Neuroscientists now understand that learning to play an instrument is one of the rare activities that activates virtually every region of the brain simultaneously. This is no small feat. We're talking about the brain's motor regions, which coordinate the movement of hands and feet; the auditory centers, which process pitch, rhythm, and tone; and the prefrontal cortex, which supports concentration, memory, and executive decision-making.

Think of your brain as a vast city, with different neighborhoods (regions) each specialized for specific tasks. Now, imagine music learning as a master urban planner, building superhighways, freeways and interconnecting roads between these neighborhoods, allowing for faster, more efficient communication. This is exactly what happens when we learn music. The corpus callosum—what I call the "creativity control center"—is the brain's main highway connecting left and right hemispheres. It actually grows larger and is more efficient in musicians. Learning music changes the structure of the brain's white matter, and it increases the amount of gray matter in different brain regions. Not only that, it increases the long-range connectivity between those regions. This enhanced connectivity isn't just an interesting scientific fact; it's a game changer for how we think, create, and solve problems.

When you're learning to play an instrument, you're not just making music—you're literally rewiring your brain for improved performance across all areas of life. These new neural highways can allow creative and analytical thoughts to flow more freely, enabling you to see multiple perspectives and generate innovative solutions to challenges, whether in business strategy sessions or personal relationships.

BUILDING COGNITIVE RESILIENCE THROUGH NEUROPLASTICITY

Jim Kwik, one of the world's leading brain coaches, describes music learning this way: "Music is the medicine of both the mind and the soul. Music stimulates not only certain brain areas; it stimulates your entire brain. It's a total brain workout."[10]

And he's absolutely right. Just as exercise strengthens muscles, music learning strengthens the brain's ability to adapt and grow—a quality scientists call neuroplasticity. This isn't just about being able to play a piece of music; it's about building a brain that's more resilient and adaptable to change. In today's rapidly evolving world, this kind of cognitive flexibility is more valuable than ever.

---

10   Jim Kwik, "The Effects of Music on Your Brain," Kwik Learning, November 19, 2018, https://kwiklearning.com/kwik-tips/the-effects-of-music-on-your-brain/.

Research shows that musicians' brains display enhanced plasticity well into adulthood, maintaining their ability to learn and adapt long after others might begin to experience cognitive decline. This increased plasticity translates directly into real-world benefits: faster learning of new skills, better adaptation to changing circumstances, and more creative approaches to problem-solving.

MEMORY ENHANCEMENT: BUILDING A MORE CAPABLE MIND

Learning music is like installing a memory upgrade in your brain. Musicians develop enhanced working memory—the mental workspace where we manipulate information—and enhanced long-term memory systems. This isn't limited to remembering music; these improvements could carry over into all aspects of life.

Consider how this enhanced memory capability might play out in professional settings: this could translate to better retention of important information, improved project management skills, and more effective relationship building through better recall of personal details and past interactions. These memory improvements aren't just about storing more information—they're about processing and using that information more effectively.

PATTERN RECOGNITION AND PREDICTIVE THINKING

Music is fundamentally about patterns—melodic patterns, harmonic patterns, rhythmic patterns. As musicians learn to recognize and work with these patterns, they develop sophisticated pattern recognition abilities that can extend far beyond music.

This enhanced pattern recognition could become a powerful tool in business, personal relationships, and problem-solving.

Imagine being able to spot market trends before others, anticipate relationship dynamics, or see solutions to complex problems by recognizing underlying patterns. This is what musicians' brains are trained to do. Their enhanced pattern-recognition abilities could support making them naturally better at strategic thinking and creative problem-solving.

EMOTIONAL INTELLIGENCE AND SOCIAL COGNITION

Music learning doesn't just develop cognitive skills—it profoundly affects our emotional and social capabilities. Playing music activates and strengthens the brain regions responsible for empathy, emotional understanding, and social connection. This enhanced emotional intelligence would be a powerful asset in both personal and professional relationships.

Musicians often develop enhanced abilities to read emotional cues, understand others' perspectives, and navigate complex social situations. These skills would lend themselves to better leadership abilities, more effective team collaboration, and stronger personal relationships.

EXECUTIVE FUNCTION AND ATTENTION

Learning music is like boot camp for your brain's executive function—the mental processes that enable us to plan, focus, remember instructions, and handle multiple tasks successfully. Musicians develop enhanced attention networks and cognitive control systems, enabling better focus, more effective multitasking, and improved decision-making under pressure.

This enhanced executive function could become particularly valuable in high-pressure professional situations, complex project management, and any scenario requiring careful attention to detail while maintaining a broader strategic perspective.

PROFESSIONAL SUCCESS

Enhanced creative problem-solving doesn't just mean thinking "outside the box"—it means reconstructing the box entirely. Musicians develop neural networks that approach challenges from multiple angles simultaneously, much like a composer who must balance a complex array of melodies, harmonies, and rhythms. In the business world, this would be analogous to having an ability to see solutions where others see only obstacles.

A "musician-tuned entrepreneur" might approach a market challenge the way they would approach a difficult passage in music: breaking it down into manageable components, trying different approaches, and ultimately finding an innovative solution that others might miss.

The leadership capabilities developed through music are particularly noteworthy. Consider how an orchestra conductor must coordinate multiple sections, each playing different parts, to create a cohesive whole. Musicians develop similar abilities, and how might this translate to "conduct" their professional teams, reading subtle cues, maintaining group cohesion, and guiding complex projects to successful completion? Enhanced leadership capacity would be supported by the brain's improved emotional processing centers, developed through years of musical interpretation and expression.

How might strategic thinking and planning abilities be dramatically enhanced through music learning? Just as musicians develop the neural framework to think ahead while playing, this is analogous to thinking several steps ahead in business strategy.

This isn't coincidental—the same brain regions that process musical structure and form are actively engaged in strategic planning and foresight.

In Craig Cortello's book *Everything We Needed to Know About Business We Learned Playing Music*, business leaders and CEOs consistently reported that their success in business, project planning, and execution was because their brain was wired to handle complex, multilayered tasks while maintaining a clear view of the ultimate goal-skills. They attribute this enhanced capability directly to their music-learning experience.

PERSONAL DEVELOPMENT

It stands to reason that the emotional intelligence fostered through music-learning becomes a cornerstone of personal growth and relationship building. Musicians develop an acute sensitivity to emotional nuance—not just in music, but in human interaction. This enhanced emotional awareness stems from the strengthened neural connections between cognitive and emotional centers in the brain. In practice, this might mean better understanding of a partner's needs in a relationship, more effective communication with family members, or stronger bonds with friends through deeper emotional comprehension. The same German study mentioned earlier found that when people study music they become more conscientious, more ambitious, and more open!

Stress management and resilience could take on new dimensions through musical training. The brain of a musician learns to maintain calm focus under pressure—a skill developed through performances and practiced through the learning process. This same neural circuitry helps manage everyday stress, from workplace deadlines to personal challenges. The ability to maintain composure under pressure becomes a natural extension of the mental discipline developed through music.

Learning capabilities expand dramatically through musical training, creating what neuroscientists call "learning to learn." The neural pathways strengthened through music practice enhance our ability to acquire new skills in any domain. A musician who takes up a new language or technical skill often progresses faster because their brain has been trained in the art of systematic learning and pattern recognition. This enhanced learning capability becomes particularly valuable in an era where continuous learning is essential for professional and personal growth.

COGNITIVE LONGEVITY

Perhaps one of the most remarkable benefits of musical training is its impact on long-term brain health. Research shows that musicians maintain stronger cognitive function as they age, developing what scientists call a "cognitive reserve." This isn't just about staying mentally sharp—it's about building a brain that resists decline. Think of it as creating a cognitive retirement account, where every hour of practice contributes to future mental resilience.

Mental flexibility throughout life becomes a natural by-product of continued musical engagement. Just as a pianist must keep their fingers nimble through regular practice, musicians maintain cognitive flexibility through the constant mental challenges of music learning and performance. This sustained flexibility helps in adapting to new technologies, social changes, and life transitions well into later years.

The enhanced lifetime learning capacity of musicians is particularly relevant in our rapidly evolving world. The brain of a lifelong musician remains more adaptable and receptive to new information, much like a well-maintained instrument that stays in tune. This capacity for continued learning doesn't just apply to music—it extends to all areas of life, from mastering new technologies to understanding changing social dynamics.

Sustained creative capabilities in later life represent another crucial advantage. Musicians often maintain their creative thinking abilities longer than nonmusicians, thanks to the enhanced neural connectivity developed through years of practice. This creativity isn't limited to artistic expression—it manifests in problem-solving, adaptation to life changes, and finding novel solutions to age-related challenges.

THE INTEGRATION EFFECT

What makes these benefits particularly powerful is their interconnected nature. The professional advantages feed into personal development, which supports cognitive longevity, creating a self-reinforcing cycle of enhanced capability. A musician who applies their pattern recognition skills in business might find those same skills helping them navigate personal relationships more effectively, while simultaneously building cognitive reserve for the future.

This integration of benefits creates what we might call a "cognitive compound interest"—where each advantage builds upon and enhances the others. The result is a brain that's not just better at specific tasks, but fundamentally more capable across all domains of life.

LIFELONG LEARNING AND EQUIPPING
YOUR BRAIN FOR THE FUTURE

As you can see, music learning is a pathway to neurological fitness—a training ground for a brain that's agile, resilient, and equipped for a world in flux. The benefits extend far beyond mere skill acquisition. Music learning provides a comprehensive mental workout, serves as critical neurological nutrition, and builds the connectivity that underlies creative capability—the brain's structural capacity for innovative thinking and creative problem-solving.

This isn't just about being more creative in an artistic sense; it's about developing the neural framework that supports innovative thinking in any context, allowing us to see things differently, think about things differently, and do things differently.

IMPACT OF MUSIC OVER A LIFETIME

The journey of a human being's life from the prenatal stage to elderhood presents a series of developmental milestones. To really understand the scope of how comprehensive and universal the benefits of music are, we must delve more deeply into an exploration of how these neurological, creative, and holistic benefits manifest across various life stages. We address this matter more fully in the Appendix section of this book, providing some insight into the impact that music-learning has over various stages of life. Here are some examples of how powerful music can be, even beginning prior to birth!

Around the twentieth week of gestation, a fetus begins to hear sounds from the outside world, and introducing music to an unborn child during this time provides stimulation to their developing brain. This stimulation aids in the auditory development of the fetus and may establish early patterns of cognition and emotion.

A study by Partanen et al. supports this notion as it found that fetuses can recognize and remember sounds from the outside world, which indicates an impact on early neural development.[11] Music intervention during the prenatal period has shown to have other significant benefits on the fetus as well.

Another study monitored the fetal heart rate and movement responses to familiar and unfamiliar music in pregnant women between thirty and thirty-eight weeks of gestational age.[12] The results revealed that unborn babies who were exposed to music while in the womb showed a significant improvement in their overall mental, cognitive, behavioral, sensory, psychological, and emotional development compared to those who were not exposed to music.

In Dr. Thomas Verny's 1982 book, *The Secret Life of the Unborn Child*, world-renowned Canadian conductor Boris Brott was asked how he had become interested in music.[13]

"You know this might sound strange," Brott answered, "but music has been a part of me since before birth. As a young man I was mystified by this unusual ability I had to play certain pieces sight unseen. I'd be conducting a score for the first time and, suddenly, the cello line would jump out at me; I'd know the flow of the piece even before I turned the page of the score.

---

11   Eino Partanen et al., "Prenatal Music Exposure Induces Long-Term Neural Effects," *PLoS One* 8, no. 10 (October 30, 2013): e78946, https://doi.org/10.1371/journal.pone.0078946.

12   Liza Lee et al., "The Effect of Music Intervention on Fetal Education via Doppler Fetal Monitor," *Children (Basel)* 9, no. 6 (June 18, 2022): 918, https://doi.org/10.3390/children9060918.

13   Thomas Verny and John Kelly, *The Secret Life of the Unborn Child* (Dell Trade, 1982),10.

"One day, I mentioned this to my mother, who is a professional cellist. I thought she'd be intrigued because it was always the cello line that was so distinct in my mind," Brott recalled. "She was intrigued, but when she heard what the pieces were, the mystery quickly solved itself. All the scores I knew, sight unseen, were the ones she had played while she was pregnant with me."

Brott heard the music while in his mother's womb and, remarkably, remembered it well enough to conduct an orchestra decades later. Brott's prenatal story demonstrates most vividly the impact of music on babies in the womb.

The modern era has brought a plethora of research underscoring the multifaceted impact of music and music education on child development, from infancy through early childhood. Engaging with music, whether it be through listening, singing, or playing instruments, fosters a rich environment for brain development, creativity nurturing, and emotional, psychological, and behavioral growth. Music education significantly contributes to early childhood development in a variety of areas: cognitive development, social and emotional development, and even physical development.

The multifaceted benefits of music education are profound and enduring, significantly enriching the early developmental stages of a child's life. It's imperative that stakeholders in education and policymaking recognize the value of music education and strive to make it accessible for every child. The harmonious blend of cognitive, creative, and emotional growth catalyzed by music education underscores its pivotal role in nurturing well-rounded, resilient, and imaginative individuals ready to embrace the challenges and opportunities of the future.

In children aged five to twelve, music education can significantly contribute to their cognitive, emotional, psychological, and behavioral growth. Music engages cognitive functions like planning, working memory, inhibition, and flexibility, known as executive functions, as well as improved mathematical abilities, including enhanced spatial-temporal skills, which can be foundational for understanding complex mathematical concepts. It can also strengthen phonological processing, which aids reading proficiency, and have positive effects on a child's social and emotional development.

There are also benefits of music education for teenagers, including cognitive, social, and emotional development, as well as a reduction in anxiety and stress and higher academic achievement.

The benefits continue into adulthood. One study found that adults engaged in music may have better cognitive flexibility, allowing them to adapt to new information or environments efficiently.

Another suggested a delay in natural cognitive decline through an increased resilience in attention, memory, and self-discipline.

Finally, for elders sixty years and above, music education and engagement present a unique array of advantages that contribute to healthy aging, both cognitively and emotionally. The profound impact of music education on elders transcends the mere act of making music. It offers a holistic approach to promoting cognitive, emotional, and social wellness, thereby significantly contributing to the quality of life and well-being of individuals in their golden years.

As in adulthood, engaging in musical activities can help elders maintain neuroplasticity, fostering the brain's ability to change and adapt. Continuous engagement with music can also help older adults retain better auditory processing abilities, crucial for understanding speech.

Musical activities may even offer some protection against dementia and Alzheimer's disease. Playing an instrument can help elders maintain and even enhance their motor skills, aiding in daily tasks. Regular practice and musical engagement can provide elders with a structured routine, which is beneficial for cognitive health. Listening to or playing music regularly can also offer emotional solace, helping elders cope with feelings of loneliness, depression, or anxiety.

Music education can also serve as a motivating activity, providing a sense of accomplishment and joy, which are essential for promoting positive psychological and behavioral outcomes among elders.

Dr. Limb sums up the overwhelming amount of evidence in support of music's ability to develop neural connectivity very simply:

> Music changes the brain. And music is such a robust stimulus for the brain that it can change it in a kind of multimodal way. There are so many ways to engage with music that it can influence your brain in several different contexts, whether it's as a professional musician or somebody who is a child or somebody who is an adult that's picking up an instrument late for the first time, or whether it's a listener or a composer or whatever it might be.[14]

A CALL TO ACTION

Clearly, the act of being involved in a musical activity has positive effects on all humans, from the womb to the end of a life. And while the studies referred to above can suggest and indicate the vast array of impacts on the human brain, the research is

---

14   Limb, interview by author.

still a work in progress. However, from the enormity of the above findings, we can at least get a clear sense of the totality of the impact that learning music is thought to have on all the developmental stages of life, in so many different areas.

My call to action is simple yet profound: Consider learning and playing music as a lifelong companion. Whether you're picking up an instrument for the first time (regardless of age), or returning to it after years away, the cognitive benefits of music will serve you in countless ways. In embracing musicianship as a means of keeping your mind strong, creative, and adaptive, you will be far better prepared and ready to tackle the unique challenges of the future.

But given the enormous benefits that arise from learning music, and given the fact that music has been taught for generations, why is it that so few people are able to play? This and many other important questions are exactly what we need to explore in our next chapter.

PART 2

A NEW ERA
IN MUSIC
EDUCATION

UNLOCKING OUR CREATIVE POTENTIAL
THROUGH PLAYING-BASED LEARNING

Chapter 5

THE FAILED CHARTER OF MUSIC EDUCATION

"One must learn by doing the thing; for though you think you know it, you have no certainty until you try."

—SOPHOCLES

THE FAILED CHARTER

I have concerns about the current state of traditional music education. I assert that, in some respects, our traditional approach has failed and continues to fail in achieving its fundamental charter: to equip the population with the ability to be musically self-expressed.

After 300 years of formal music education, only a tiny fraction of the population can play music. There are vast numbers of students who begin lessons and quit before ever really learning how to play. A great many who persist commonly find the experience joyless and abandon music as soon as they stop taking lessons. The enormous extent of this failing provides us with the opportunity to ask some critical questions:

- Have we succeeded in fulfilling our fundamental charter of equipping the population with the ability to be musically self-expressed? If not, why not?
- Do all (or at very least, mostly all) students of all ages, who begin music lessons, develop and nurture a deep connection to their natural musicality, acquire the ability to play, and maximize the likelihood of having musicianship in their lives for the rest of their lives? If not, why not?
- Have we created a culture where every person is absolutely, positively clear about the fact that all human beings, without exception, are deeply, naturally, and profoundly musical? If not, why not?
- Have we fully and completely dispelled the nonsense, myths, and illusions surrounding music learning and musicality itself, such as:
    - Learning to play an instrument is hard;
    - Learning to play music takes a long time;
    - You have to start learning music when you are young;
    - Some people have "musical talent" and others don't;
    - You must have formal music education in order to teach music.
- If we've not yet dispelled these notions, why not?

There is no doubt that traditional music education has contributed enormously to world culture. It's created many brilliant music educators, as well as extraordinary musicians who have entertained us and preserved the works of history's greatest composers. Even so, it remains a fact that:

- Only a tiny fraction of the population has the ability to play music. Why is this?
- The majority of students who begin music lessons quit long before they ever acquire the ability to play. Why is this?
- Far too many students having music lessons don't enjoy the experience and stop playing music as soon as they quit having lessons. Why is this?
- Far too many highly trained and formally credentialed music educators blame the student for the lack of progress and absence of satisfying results. Why is this?

I've found, time and time again, that the typical answers that many music educators provide when responding to these questions center around a strongly held belief that the student is at "fault" and/or there is something "missing" in the student—some apparent lack of discipline, or commitment, or ability, or talent, or focus, etc., etc. These typical answers, in my opinion, don't even remotely come close to addressing the matter, nor do they begin to get to the heart of the problem.

THE ORIGINS OF DISCONNECT

To understand how we arrived here, we must trace the history of how music education evolved from natural expression to complex notation. Looking back through history reveals a fascinating yet troubling transformation: What began as an intuitive, sound-based approach to musical learning gradually evolved into a system that prioritizes theoretical knowledge and notation over musical self-expression.

Before the formalization of music education, learning was predominantly based on what educators now call the "sound before symbol" approach. The evidence is compelling: Wolfgang Amadeus Mozart was playing keyboard by age three and composing by age five, yet he didn't learn to notate his own music until age six. Johannes Brahms learned informally at home until age seven, only starting formal lessons then, and theory at age ten. Béla Bartók showed musical aptitude at eighteen months and was playing piano by ear at age four, with formal instruction coming later.

This natural progression—listening, playing, and only later learning notation—was the standard approach for generations. Musicians developed through a combination of aural learning, improvisation, and practical experimentation with their instruments. The emphasis was on musical expression and understanding, with technical skills and notation serving as tools rather than primary focus areas.

The story of disconnect may well begin in ancient Greece, where the discovery that halving a vibrating string created predictable pitch relationships. This discovery, in all likelihood, is what led to the exploration of music as seen through a mathematical lens. While this mathematical correlation gave music scientific validity, it began a separation between music as natural expression and music as theoretical construct. And while music can be explained mathematically, it doesn't belong there.

This divide widened dramatically in medieval times. When Guido of Arezzo developed early music notation around AD 1025, his goal was preservation—creating a way to record and transmit sacred chants. This system of notation, while brilliant for preservation, was not necessarily intended as a method for learning music. Yet somehow, over centuries, learning to read notation became the gateway to learning music itself.

THE GREAT REVERSAL

The transformation began in earnest during the mid-nineteenth century, driven by several societal changes. The rise of the middle class and widespread availability of pianos created an unprecedented demand for music education. The establishment of conservatories, formal examination systems, and the professionalization of music teaching led to standardized assessment methods. By the 1920s and 1930s, the examination grade system had become so dominant that many teachers exclusively taught the exam syllabus.

This emphasis on notation marks one of history's great educational reversals. In preindustrial cultures and many non-Western societies today, music remains deeply integrated into daily life. Some cultures don't even have separate words for walking, dancing, singing, and playing—they're all considered one natural human activity. Music was learned as language: through immersion, imitation, discovery, and natural expression.

The Western formalization of music education changed this natural order. Just as medieval scholars restricted literacy to those who could master Latin, music education became the domain of elites who could decipher complex notation. This system, born in the Dark Ages, persists today. Had recording technology existed 500 years ago, our approach to music education might be radically different.

THE NEUROLOGICAL MISMATCH

What traditional music education appears to have failed to recognize is its fundamental misalignment with how the human brain functions. Research indicates that the brain is a single-thought processing device, yet traditional methods demand multiple simultaneous processes:

- Reading complex notation
- Maintaining precise technical form
- Processing theoretical concepts
- Executing perfect performance[15]

This creates an intense cognitive burden, especially for beginners. It's like teaching someone to walk by first requiring them to understand anatomy, physics, and biomechanics. Or teaching cooking by starting with molecular gastronomy rather than by simply making food.

THE LANGUAGE PARALLEL

Consider how we learn language: Children speak for years before reading or understanding grammar. They babble, make mistakes, and gradually refine their abilities through practice and immersion. No one expects accurate pronunciation from a toddler learning to speak. No one requires understanding of syntax before allowing verbal expression. It's clearly understood that the *quantity* of their vocabulary is the vehicle that, over years, organically elevates the *quality* of their vocabulary.

In reality, we lovingly interact with a young child's babbling attempts at verbalization as being delightful, amusing, entertaining, beautiful, and a naturally organic progression. It wouldn't occur to us to relate to our child's early stages of language acquisition as being mistaken, erroneous, and in need of constant correction.

In fact, if we were to take our current, traditional approach

---

15   "Why Multitasking Does More Harm than Good," Wu Tsai Neurosciences Institute, May 10, 2021, https://neuroscience.stanford.edu/news/why-multitasking-does-more-harm-good?utm_source=chatgpt.com.

to music education, where students are required to learn how to read music as a means of learning how to play, and then apply that to natural language acquisition, we would now expect children to learn how to spell and read as a means of learning how to speak. What a preposterous idea!

Yet in music, we do exactly this. We place high priority on technical perfection before allowing creative expression. We insist on theoretical understanding before permitting play. We require reading proficiency before allowing musical speech. This approach contradicts everything we know about natural learning processes.

Historical evidence supports this parallel. Legendary musicians of the past learned through what we now call the "sound before symbol" approach. Concert pianist Andor Földes wrote in 1950: "There is no such thing as a proper age for a child to start playing the piano. I avoid saying 'to start his musical education' because I believe that an education in music should start very early, perhaps years before the child ever actually learns how to read notes."[16]

"Simply Music has broken the mold and set a new standard for what can be accomplished in a very short period of time."

—MICHELLE MASONER (BOARD MEMBER, SACRAMENTO BOARD OF EDUCATION)

---

16   Andor Foldes, *Keys to the Keyboard* (Oxford University Press, 1950), 20.

THE HUMAN COST

The consequences of this failed approach have been more than significant. I remember one story, of a vast multitude that I've heard over decades, where an adult student showed me tattoo-like marks on his hand. They weren't tattoos, but permanent markings from a teacher who would stab his hand with a sharpened pencil for every "mistake" he made. I've heard countless stories from students who have been struck by teachers, yelled at by teachers, psychologically humiliated by teachers, publicly chastised by teachers—for no reason other than making errors in the early stages of their lessons. While such physical abuse is perhaps rarer today, the psychological damage continues. To this day, when we inherit students who have had prior traditional experience, we commonly see them flinch at the piano when they make an "error"—muscle memory from being struck or verbally abused for playing "wrong" notes. Today, the wounding is more subtle but equally destructive.

"I fired a student today," a teacher announces proudly. "Your son has no musical ability—stick to sports," another tells a parent. These casual dismissals silence musical voices forever. In classrooms, students face public humiliation, forced to repeat-sing a line before judging peers, without any foundation in their natural musicality. It's like throwing nonswimmers into deep water and declaring them permanently unsuited for swimming when they struggle.

THE CYCLE OF ELITISM

Over the decades I've navigated the world of music education, I've been struck by the way traditional systems often perpetuate themselves. Time and again, I've seen the same pattern unfold: A student endures the rigors and criticisms of traditional training, internalizing the belief that musical achievement requires years of struggle, discipline, and even suffering. They emerge, often bruised if not scarred, but also invested in their identity as one of the musical "elite." And then, all too often, they go on to become teachers themselves, re-creating for their own students the same punishing system that shaped them. It's a cycle that I've come to see as not only unfortunate but deeply counterproductive. Because in positioning musical mastery as the result of struggle and hardship, we close the door to the sheer pleasure and creative expression that music, at its best, can unleash.

This cycle likely began solidifying in the late nineteenth century when music education became increasingly professionalized. Conservatories were founded, professional qualifications were created, and formal "graded exam" assessments became a booming business. By the early twentieth century, the emphasis had shifted dramatically toward technical perfection and theoretical knowledge, often at the expense of musical expression and enjoyment.

RETHINKING "MUSICAL ABILITY"

What about innate ability? While people clearly display different levels of proficiency—not every walker becomes an Olympic athlete—the relationship between ability and achievement is more paradoxical than it appears. I regularly witnessed this on numerous occasions. For example, in one instance I began teaching two young girls who were best friends and could have been twins. They were the same age, same height and build, both with blonde hair, and had similar mannerisms. In their very first lesson, one immediately grasped a two-handed piece and was playing it, using both hands, within minutes. The other stared at her fingers, trying to will them to move, but apparently getting nowhere. This wasn't a difference in musicality or potential—it was simply that the first girl's neural pathways were already and more readily connected. Her friend's brain hadn't yet established the connections to channel her equally innate musicality to her fingers—a temporary state that would quickly change.

Does "innate ability" or talent exist? Certainly, some people demonstrate extraordinary natural gifts that, when nurtured, can lead to prodigy-level achievement. But focusing on exceptional talent misses the larger truth: Musicality is universal. My vision isn't about focusing on creating concert-level, nor exceptional, nor even advanced musicianship—it's about everyone acquiring, experiencing, and retaining music as a lifelong companion. This aligns with what I believe should be the fundamental charter of music education: equipping all people with musical self-expression.

"I am a Clinical Professor of Psychiatry at UCLA, and an adult and child psychiatrist and psychoanalyst in private practice. I am seventy-five years old. I had taken a few lessons from my piano teacher mother when I was a child. That was a dismal failure. I hated taking lessons. I found it to be difficult and was convinced that I had no talent and that I was wasting my time. I quit.

Since beginning Simply Music, a whole new world has opened up for me. I find this program easy, fun and very rewarding. I didn't think I had any talent, but now I feel I do. I can't stay away from the piano. In a week our piano will be overhauled and out of commission for five days. I am already feeling anxious about the loss of my instrument.

The piano has become so important to me that I've rearranged my priorities. It has helped to sharpen my memory and mental capacities. My manual dexterity has improved. I believe that everyone, child, adult or senior, who has ever had any wish to play an instrument should consider Simply Music."

—WALTER E. BRACKELMANNS, MD (SIMPLY MUSIC STUDENT)

LEARNING THROUGH NATURAL EXPRESSION

Consider how children learn to cook. When teaching a child to make lasagna, we don't begin with knife theory, ingredient chemistry, or the physics of heat transfer. We simply let them cook, offering guidance when needed. Some may show more natural aptitude, but that's not the point—making lasagna is.

Language acquisition follows the same pattern. Parents don't teach grammar rules or vocal cord physics—they simply create an environment rich in language. Through natural exposure and expression, nearly every child learns to speak. They don't all speak the same way. In spoken language we hear massive differences in accents and pronunciation. Some have a vast vocabulary; others have a vocabulary that's no larger than what was learned in the early years of grade school. But that's irrelevant; what matters is that they acquire language—however basic—and can express themselves.

Music learning should follow this natural pattern. When we force it into a technical, theoretical, mathematical framework, we create disconnect from our intuitive musical nature. If you've ever thought, "I'm not musical," remember: It's impossible to be human and not be musical. The problem isn't lack of ability—it's the approach that conflicts with our natural way of learning and being.

THE NEURAL DISCONNECT

Traditional music education doesn't just fail pedagogically—it works against our neurological design. The brain, by design, is a pattern-seeking device, yet in traditional methods we force it to process multiple, mathematical, technical, and theoretical concepts simultaneously. We require complex translation of symbols before allowing simple expression of sound—music notation is actually a multisymbolic language, with completely distinct sets of symbols for pitch, rhythm, region, expression and dynamics, pedalling, fingering, and, of course, lyrics. If we were to be genuinely more rigorous about it, we would not call it "reading music"; we would call it "simultaneous multiple-language translation."

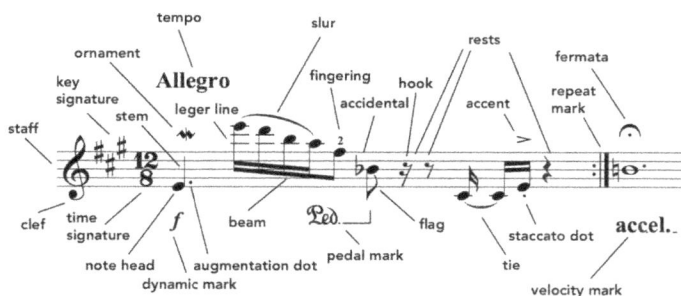

An example of the many different types of symbols commonly used in music notation

This is far beyond just being inefficient—it's fundamentally misaligned to the way the brain processes information, and it actively contributes to creating a disconnect to one's profound and natural musicality. As you might expect when forcing unnatural processes, the neural wires get crossed. Instead of strengthening natural musical pathways, we establish the psychological habit of struggle, difficulty, and failure, and as a result, we create confusion, resistance, and resignation. The brain, designed for single-thought processing, rebels against this multitasking demand, leading to tension, anxiety, and often, a complete shutdown of musical instincts.

THE NEED FOR TRANSFORMATION

Traditional methods of music teaching have clearly played an important role throughout traditional times, but we're now far from traditional times. What's urgently needed, in this day and age, is a breakthrough in music education. As we stand at the threshold of unprecedented technological change, we urgently need a new era of music education. Our approach must acknowledge and build upon two fundamental truths: All humans are naturally musical, and our brains are pattern-seeking devices.

What's urgently needed, in this day and age, is a breakthrough in music education. Humanity is at the threshold of witnessing the arrival of a technological tsunami that will, forevermore, alter the experience of what it means to be human. Now, more so than ever, we're in dire need of a new era of music education—one that's founded on the premise and acknowledgement of the fact that all human beings are deeply and naturally musical.

We need:

- a system of music education that immediately connects students (of all ages) with their deep and innate musicianship.
- a methodology that has students playing great-sounding music—immediately—from their very first lessons.
- music education that's designed to serve the wants and needs of the population at large—an approach that's designed to nurture and celebrate the populations of people who simply want to play for fun, for recreation, for therapy, for companionship, for personal entertainment, for self-expression, for solace and comfort, for the sheer and simple love of music.
- a system of learning that easily and immediately contributes to those who play as a means of interacting with and managing their special needs and/or complex learning differences.
- a method of learning that's specifically designed for the

multitudes—the populations of people who will never be (nor would ever want to be) "advanced" musicians, but who simply want to experience the pleasure of playing music and having it as a companion in their lives.

- a system that allows students to establish the psychological habit of success and victory, that teaches students how to successfully navigate long-term relationships, and that helps develop life-enhancement skills.

- a system that focuses on using music learning as a means of developing patience and self-acceptance, and that celebrates the importance of incremental gratification, partnership, and collaboration.

- Of even perhaps greatest importance, we need a system of music education that understands the power of using music as a means of providing critical neurological nutrition that stimulates our fundamental creative capability.

"This is a wonderful music program and the results are astounding! Even if you don't consider yourself musically talented, this program is designed for you! It is easy to understand and easy to play a full repertoire of beautiful songs from a variety of genres. I also think this program could be a major breakthrough for children with a variety of cognitive delays and learning disabilities. I love the Simply Music approach."

—DR. ANNE MARGARET WRIGHT (PSYD, EDUCATIONAL CONSULTANT, *THE OLD SCHOOLHOUSE MAGAZINE*)

REDEFINING "MUSIC TEACHER"

There is another equally important issue that we need to address here and that's the need for us to culturally redefine who's capable of successfully teaching music. If we're to truly democratize music education and unlock humanity's creative potential, we must revolutionize not just how music is learned, but who can teach it. The breakthrough we seek requires dual transformations: in our teaching methods and in our concept of who qualifies as a teacher. Our current system, which demands extensive formal training and advanced musical capability from educators, creates an artificial bottleneck that severely restricts access to musical learning.

Consider again the parallel with language acquisition: Parents successfully guide their children into complex linguistic expression but don't require that they hold degrees or advanced capability in grammar, elocution, or linguistics. Parents achieve this quite thoughtlessly—it's far more so the result of intuitive understanding, loving encouragement, and natural interaction. Similarly, we need a music education system that's designed for the masses, and that empowers a broader spectrum of teachers—individuals who may not be advanced musicians or concert-level performers, do not necessarily have formal qualifications, and may even be relatively new to playing themselves, but who possess the essential qualities of empathy, communication skills, and a deep love for both music and teaching.

The gateway to musical expression can't be guarded solely by traditionally credentialed educators. If we truly believe in accessibility, we must expand our vision of who can effectively guide others on their musical journey. This means recognizing that teaching ability isn't solely determined by performance capability or theoretical knowledge, but by the capacity to communicate, connect, inspire, and guide. This cultural shift in redefining music teachers is as crucial as the methodological transformation itself—perhaps even more so, as it holds the key to truly widespread access to musical self-expression.

WHO IS CAPABLE OF TEACHING?

Being a great teacher requires an entirely different skillset than what can be provided by mere formal education and advanced performance. Decades of evidence proves this to be a fact. There are scores of highly advanced and formally trained musicians who, quite simply, don't have the personal skills nor mindset to be good educators. (And, frankly, we know this to be true across a multitude of fields of endeavor.)

Having said that, and having had the opportunity to personally train thousands of music educators, I've had decades of firsthand experience in working with scores of people who don't have a degree in music, who aren't advanced players, nor have they had years of teaching experience, but who do possess a deep and intuitive relationship to the nature of learning, who love music, who love people, who understand the dynamics and subtleties of communication, who are uniquely open-minded to new perspectives and new ways of learning, who have the ability to guide and direct and mentor people (of all ages), and who can learn and be trained in the practicality, the psychology, and the behavioral mechanics that are at play when teaching.

If the goal is to truly democratize music education and open the doors for musical self-expression to be accessible for the masses (which I believe it should be), then it's time for us to usher in a new era of music learning. It's time for us to open our minds, our hearts, and our hands, and embrace simpler approaches that are far less formal, less technical, and less demanding. We need to shift our focus and attention away from the judgment of "how" people play, and place far greater importance on "that" people play.

"A twist of events changed my life forever. As an adult, playing the piano has always been my dream, but I didn't think it was possible. Then, I came across Simply Music, intending to teach it to my children. I discovered that I loved playing the piano and wanted to express myself. The music inside of me came alive. As a novice piano player, it never even crossed my mind to consider teaching music. Now, after two decades, I'm living my dream of playing the piano, and have built and maintained a successful, thriving music studio."

—BERNADETTE ASHBY (SIMPLY MUSIC TEACHER)

THE PATH FORWARD

Music theory, advanced technique, and reading and writing music are clearly valuable skills and knowledge—but not as starting points. Just as we let children speak before teaching them to read, we must let people play before introducing the more formal aspects of more advanced musicianship. Music should be a pleasant, wonderful experience free from the burden of more advanced principles of technique or theoretical understanding. Students need a broad musical vocabulary, just as children need many words—but this comes through playing, not drilling.

This isn't about lowering standards—it's about changing priorities. **The issue isn't about how well someone plays, but whether they play at all.** When we focus on that, instead of technical excellence, something remarkable can happen: Not only would it create a world where vastly more people are playing, but eventually this will translate to there being a far larger pool of musicians who are eager, anxious, and desirous of achieving higher levels of musicianship through more formal development.

In playing the long game, it's a win–win all around.

A NEW CHARTER FOR A NEW ERA

As we face a future where creative thinking becomes increasingly crucial, we must transform music education from an elite pursuit into a universal language of creative expression. We need approaches that:

- build neural connectivity through natural musical engagement.
- develop creative capability through actual playing and improvising.
- emphasize finding a balance between guidance and discovery.
- foster success experiences rather than criticism.
- create lifelong relationships with music.
- support broader cognitive and creative development.

The evidence is clear: Musicianship develops our creative machinery, but only if we exercise it through actual expression. If we continue to require beginning students to learn how to read music as a means of learning how to play music, along with requiring theoretical and technical excellence before allowing musical expression, we not only fail our fundamental charter—we fail humanity itself.

The time has come to democratize music education, making it accessible to everyone. This isn't just about preserving great compositions; it's about preserving humanity's natural relationship with music. As we enter an era of unprecedented technological change, this transformation becomes not just desirable but essential.

We must move beyond the traditional model of music education toward something that reflects our understanding of how humans naturally learn and grow. The future demands not just musicians but creative thinkers. Through transformed music education, we can develop both—not for the gifted few, but for everyone.

It would go a long way in supporting us if we were to truly and constantly remind ourselves that music is a language. It's fundamental to the self-expression of human beings. As such, if we were to be as relaxed about music learning as we are about children learning to speak, then an extraordinary opportunity would be available to us. We might actually discover that we have, within our grasp, the opportunity to cause a breakthrough in access to musical self-expression, contribute to elevating the creative capability of humanity and, in doing so, discover a pathway for humanity to flourish in the extraordinary future we will be facing.

"Simply Music fills in the gaps for what I wasn't exposed to in the traditional world. The variety of music, the emphasis on creativity, the ability to play without relying on sheet music, improvisation and composition and accompaniment skills—those are the things that take you from being a pianist to being a truly well-rounded musician."

—GIANA NGUYEN (SIMPLY MUSIC TEACHER)

Chapter 6

THE GENESIS OF SIMPLY MUSIC

"The two most important days in life are the day you are born and the day you find out why."

—MARK TWAIN

A MUSICAL BEGINNING

The origins of Simply Music began before I was born. I believe I was instilled with a special relationship to music—one that was evident before I was even aware of my own existence. My earliest memories include feeling that I "belonged" to music, and I believe I was born with this purpose.

As the youngest of five children, with only seven years separating us all, I grew up in a home already filled with music. Each of my three brothers began piano lessons at age seven (my sister studied elocution), and my father was a singer. By the time I was born, music permeated our home—being learned, practiced, played, and performed.

There's something unique about growing up in a home where music is being learned, as distinct from one where it's simply being played. I heard the minutiae—the step-by-step progress of each note being learned and added as pieces were constructed. I experienced the birth, development, and creation of music. This intimate exposure to the learning process profoundly shaped who I am.

EARLY SIGNS

According to my parents, from infancy my relationship with music differed noticeably from my siblings'. Whether piano, record player, or radio, I would physically turn toward the sound and remain transfixed. With nine people in our home—including my uncle and grandmother—my mother had seemingly endless washing and ironing for our school uniforms. She would place me near the record player, where I would lie mesmerized, letting the music saturate me.

By age two, I could name any song from our large collection of vinyl "45s" by its very first note. More surprisingly, I could distinguish between records from the same companies—despite their nearly identical labels—and name each song correctly, even though I couldn't read. Looking back, I realize I had developed an innate ability to correlate the sound of each song with the shape of its title on the label.

THE "MUSIC AS SHAPES" CONNECTION

Within a few years, this relationship with music evolved into something more defined. Around age four, I began experiencing music visually—seeing melodies as physical shapes and patterns in my mind's eye. This wasn't something I thought about or tried to do; it happened organically, as natural as breathing.

By age seven, when I began piano lessons, this "music and shapes" relationship had solidified. As I learned new pieces, I would watch my hands moving across the keyboard and see the notes I was playing unfolding in patterns. Unlike my brothers, who learned traditionally by reading music first, I found musical notation intimidating. The written notes looked complicated and aggressive, triggering an unpleasant neurological response. More importantly, to me it seemed unnecessary—my entire approach to musicianship developed through this natural relationship with shapes and patterns.

"I have seen a lot of music programs over the years. Some were fun. Some were clever. Some were thorough. Here's one that has it all. In terms of presentation, effectiveness, philosophy—you name it—there's nothing out there that compares at all."

—MARY PRIDE
(PUBLISHER, *PRACTICAL HOMESCHOOL MAGAZINE*)

MY MUSIC LESSON EXPERIENCE

This unconventional approach, however, came with emotional complexity. I lived with constant shame, believing I was doing something wrong by not learning to read music, and fear that my "secret" would be discovered and I would face punishment.

My weekly lessons with my teacher, Frank Forbes, followed

a pattern: He would play the piece I was to learn, my well-developed ear would remember it, and as I reconstructed and practiced the piece, I would translate it into shapes and patterns. I could learn and play pieces well, but as each Saturday lesson approached, my anxiety would build. During my Saturday morning lessons, as I played for my teacher, I would stare blankly at the page, pretending to read, hoping to fool him.

What I didn't know then was that Frank would tell my mother, "Neil's not reading, he's just pretending to. He thinks he's fooling me, but he's not." My mother's wisdom in responding, "Yes, but listen to how well he's playing. Let's just leave him be and let him do his own thing," proved crucial. My ear was developed, and my "playing-based" perspective allowed me to learn and expand my musicianship in my own way.

I remain eternally grateful to both my mother for not forcing compliance with traditional methods, and to Frank for allowing me to progress naturally. I am certain that Simply Music would not exist today had my mother, or Frank, insisted on a traditional approach. Frank remained my teacher from the age of seven until I was fifteen. Why I discontinued lessons with him is another story, for perhaps another time.

THE JOURNEY TO FORMAL LEARNING

As I entered my later teens, I became increasingly aware that my inability to read music and lack of technical theory created limitations. I felt like I needed to acquire these traditional tools, but finding the right learning environment proved challenging.

Over the next fifteen years, I made several attempts to restart music lessons. Teachers who heard me play would assume a level of formal training I didn't possess, teaching at a theoretical level beyond my comprehension. These experiences left me feeling inadequate and confused. Alternatively, when teachers understood my limitations, they insisted I start from the beginning—an approach that felt wrong given that in some areas, I was already more advanced than they were. Neither scenario worked, yet I remained certain that I "belonged" to music. I couldn't articulate what "doing music" meant exactly, but I knew it was my future.

THE BUSINESS DETOUR

Being Australian presented its own challenges. While Australia matches the United States in physical size, its smaller population meant fewer opportunities, especially in music careers. Like my brothers, I didn't attend university—it wasn't our world. In my family, business was the path forward.

My wife and I bought our first restaurant in our early twenties, during the early 1980s. My plan seemed simple: earn enough money to retire early, then "do" music. The restaurant succeeded—I was passionate about food, built strong relationships with our clientele, and created a solid business. Yet something felt deeply wrong.

Over the next dozen years, my wife and I operated several businesses. While experiencing some success, I felt perpetually dissatisfied. Financial decisions weren't my strength, and after a series of poor choices on my part, we faced complete financial collapse.

THE TURNING POINT

During that time, there was one particular day where I had a powerful insight. I actually pictured my life as an equation: I'd been pursuing business, to earn money to one day do what I love. I realized that, for me, this equation was fundamentally broken. I committed, from that day forward, to pursuing what I loved and what I felt called to do. If Divine Design existed, I would trust in that, and a path would be revealed. I had no idea what that pathway would be. I was bankrupt, with my wife and our three children. I clearly remember a morning when I opened my refrigerator door, my three children were standing next to me, and there was no food there. That day, I sold my wedding jewelry at a pawn shop to feed my children.

THE FIRST STEP FORWARD

But still I knew I was going to find a way to work in music. It seemed crazy—how could I possibly work in music when I had a family to take care of? Only days later, the phone rang. It was a man whom I did know but, at that time, didn't know well. Our paths had crossed because of mutual interests and mutual friends. He said that he knew the difficulty that we were going through, and he made an extraordinary offer to support me in buying another business. It felt like a miracle, and I took it as a sign. I felt it was what I was meant to do.

I realized the business had to be simple enough that my wife and I could run it, as we had run our restaurant before she had our children. Since all of my family are self-employed, we had an understanding of running a small business. There was a restaurant in a food court of a busy shopping center. It was a small but good business that would be simple to run. Over the next year I set the business up, had it running smoothly and profitably, and it freed me up to pursue my calling. I decided that it was now time for me to learn the formal language of music. I needed to educate myself on some of the fundamentals of the theory underscoring music education.

It just so happened that the Victorian College of the Arts (which I would ordinarily have never qualified to get into), started offering weekend courses to the general public. I did three years of classical theory studies in a year, and I took some jazz improvisation studies. I didn't have an instrument; however, I called around to everyone I knew and asked if they had a piano they weren't using that I could borrow for a while.

One of the people I called was a woman I knew who told me that her brother was teaching a traditional, reading-based method he had developed that used an alternative approach. He was looking to expand the number of teachers offering his method. I took his course and gravitated to it instantly. I already had the musical foundation, I quickly learned the rudiments of his reading-based approach, and I also knew I had the ability to successfully teach this to others. It was instantly clear to me that there was an opportunity here to not only explore and develop my own playing, but also to have it be a means of generating income within the world of musicianship. I could finally "do" music.

My existing music skills, coupled with my skills in small business, prepared me to teach this approach. Looking at his system I saw that he needed help structuring his ideas into a curriculum, and I like structure. I know how to arrange minutiae. I was able to take his fragmented, scattered ideas and organize them into lesson plans. When the owner's wife died suddenly of brain cancer, he decided to take his company to America. My wife and I had always dreamed about living in America. She had become enamored with it when she spent a year in the USA as an exchange student, and I was very drawn to the amazing music coming out of that country, especially all of the jazz.

THE PATHWAY UNFOLDS

In 1994, we migrated to the United States—my wife, three children, and I—with five thousand dollars and our lives packed into three suitcases. I took a risk, investing most of our money in a newspaper ad for piano lessons. The gamble paid off; calls came in, and within months, I had built a reputation as an excellent teacher with a thriving studio, still teaching the traditional reading-based program.

My life story took a dramatic turn one day during this period. I received a call from someone at what I believe was a government agency who told me they were working with an eight-year-old boy by the name of Wade. He was blind, and was regularly in hospital having various procedures. It was very tough on him, and they wanted him to have some activity in his life that would add an element of fun. I jumped at the opportunity at first. It sounded so exciting, until I realized that the only way I knew how to teach was the reading-based approach, and this boy was blind. At that point in time I had no idea whatsoever as to how a person who was blind could learn how to read. What the heck was I going to do?

Obviously, I knew that I had never learned to read music as a child, but until that very moment it had never consciously occurred to me to ask myself the question, "What was I actually doing? How was I actually learning to play if I wasn't getting instructions from the page?" To this day I find it so strange that it had never occurred to me to actually analyze the way that I learned. It was so organic and invisible to me that I was oblivious to it. In life there is such a fine line between oblivious and obvious.

THE CRUCIBLE MOMENT

So, I began to think about it. I sat down at the piano, thought of a song, and asked myself, "How would I have learned this?" And as I went through the process, I began, for the very first time, to describe and bring language to the process of exactly what it was that I was doing. I could see it all, and explain it all, in terms of shapes and patterns that I'd organized in a specific order—simple! It might sound obscure as I explain it here, but that's how I built my musicianship over my lifetime.

This was the first time that I'd ever been able to consciously consider my approach. Prior to this, it had just been woven into my DNA. I began creating a vocabulary that would describe how I learned and how I play. I also felt very confident that I could show this boy how to position his hands, and help him feel the shapes and patterns of the notes and chords that made up any given piece. It was worth a try. I did exactly that. I just showed him how to play. He learned the song, so I showed him the next song. He learned that song the next week, and we kept at it. I was impacted by the level of success he was experiencing.

He was doing great, and I thought maybe it was because he was blind and as a result had a very "developed ear." After about three months of lessons, he had a terrific repertoire of music, and I asked his dad one day, "Are you happy with Wade's progress?" His dad told me that not only were they happy, but Wade had begun teaching his four-year-old sister how to play, and that she was also blind!

That, for me, was a crucible moment.

In that moment I realized that something very big had just happened. I didn't know what it was, but I knew that something significant had just occurred. Over the next couple of days I began to wonder what would happen if I showed all my students this approach. I imagined it might be this cool little "musical preschool" we could do before students started "real music," which I still thought was the traditional, reading-based approach I was teaching.

I started testing the approach with a few of my students, and I was shocked at how quickly and easily they were learning, as compared to what we had been doing. I was impacted by how different their learning experience was. Students became more excited about learning music. I had parents tell me that children who were previously putting up a fight about practicing now wouldn't stop practicing long enough to come to the dinner table.

"Not only has Simply Music impacted the world, but it has touched my life and the lives of each of my family members. I had no idea when I first came across it that this program would absolutely change the course of my life."

—TARASINE BUCK (SIMPLY MUSIC STUDENT)

THE BIRTH OF SIMPLY MUSIC

At that time, I figured that I was getting these results because this approach was so natural and organic to me. But I wondered what would happen if I shared this approach with other teachers. What might their experience be? In fact, they were amazed at how fast, easy, and simple it was. It was revolutionary to see the difference in how naturally their students were learning.

After that I went into deep focus mode. People often remark

that I'm very driven. I'm not driven. I'm pulled. I'm drawn. When something strikes me as an exciting breakthrough idea, I can articulate it into existence with such clarity that it creates a gravity I'm just compelled toward.

I had two primary questions in mind. Could I apply this approach to contemporary pieces, and classical, and blues etc.? And, how far could I take this approach before students needed to learn music reading and theory in order to progress?

Fortunately, at that time, I had a very full complement of students—children through elders, and at varying levels of musicianship. I was teaching weekly, private lessons, and had 125 students—it equated to me teaching around sixty-five hours a week. Every ten weeks I had taught another 1,250 lessons with the mission of building this method and figuring out how to arrange and construct it. I would present content to students, and I continued to get feedback on their experience to learn what was working and what could be done even better. This played a major role in helping me develop the program as I continued to organize, reorganize, and structure it into a curriculum. And this is how Simply Music was built—experientially, in much the same way as we teach our students to play.

MUSIC AS SHAPES AND PATTERNS

When I talk to people about my relationship to music, and how I see it in terms of shapes and patterns, it's common for them to assume that what I am describing is synesthesia—the state of experiencing a sensory "crossover"—like tasting numbers, or feeling colors—where two or more senses are activated when there's only a reason for one sense to activate.

I believe my case is very different. For me, the music–shape relationship is more so about looking at music through a particular lens, and from a specific point of view. In my case, I can describe my point of view in a way that allows others to see music through the same lens as I do. I also discovered that in learning how to see music through this lens, it could transform how quickly and easily people could learn how to play music.

Perhaps it makes most sense here for me to provide you with a few simple examples of what I mean when I talk about seeing music in terms of "shapes" and "patterns." For those of you who have had no musical training whatsoever, there might be certain things that you don't understand with regard to what I show here, but over the next few minutes I believe you'll grasp the concept of what I'm talking about.

As an analogy, consider the evening sky. We look up and see a plethora of stars, randomly scattered. But if someone points to several stars and asks you to imagine connecting the dots, we can draw a constellation—a shape.

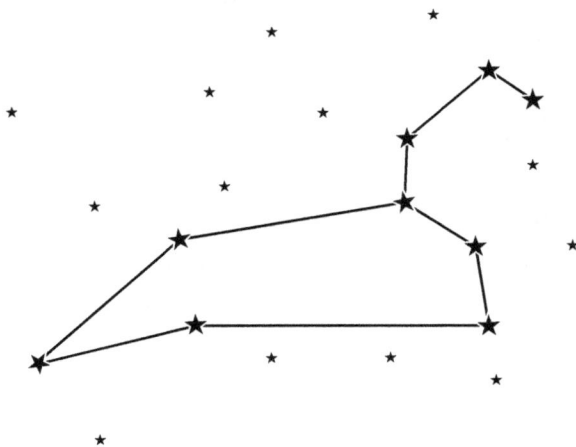

Leo

This is very much like what happens when we look at the notes played on the piano. Think of one note being played, followed by another, and again another, and then connecting those notes with an imaginary line—just like a constellation. Doing this oftentimes allows us to distinguish a series of notes as a "shape" or a "pattern."

Remember, the brain by design is a pattern-seeking device, and whenever something can be presented to the brain in the form of a shape or pattern, the brain recognizes and assimilates this very naturally and easily.

Without getting into too much detail, let me provide you with just a few specific examples of what I'm talking about.

"Let me begin by saying just how thrilled I am with the Simply Music program. I'm playing better now than I did after years of traditional lessons. I hope you provide ever more advanced studies for a long, long time to come"

—STEVE MANUEL (EXECUTIVE PRODUCER, PRIME TIME DISCOVERY CHANNEL. SIMPLY MUSIC STUDENT)

EXAMPLE 1: "ODE TO JOY"

Let's take a quick look at the first part of the melody of Beethoven's classic "Ode to Joy." The music notation would look like this:

When translated onto the piano keyboard, the melody in the above notation would unfold over five specific notes, as indicated below:

You will also notice above that I've referenced three notes in particular. The note marked "B" is what I'll call the "Bottom." The note marked "M" is what I'll call the "Middle," and the note marked "T" is what I'll call the "Top."

Played as per the music notation above, the melody would start on the Middle note, work its way up to the Top note, head all the way down to the Bottom note, then work upwards back to the Middle note.

In other words: Middle, to Top, to Bottom, to Middle—as per the diagram below:

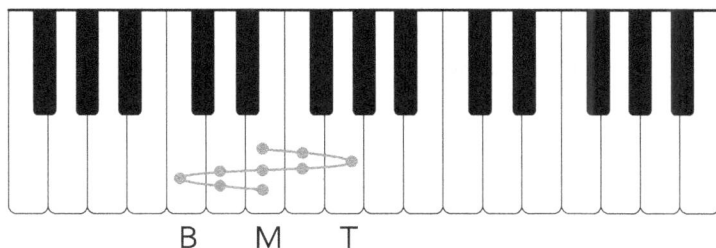

As you can see, using our "constellation" concept—joining the dots—the first part of the melody of Beethoven's "Ode to Joy" can be reduced to a simple shape:

It's eye-opening to see how quickly students are able to learn to play this piece, with both hands, when we can utilize the brain's preferred method of perception: via patterns and shapes.

EXAMPLE 2: THE BLUES SCALE

The following description will likely make little to no sense whatsoever for those of you who have had no musical background. Even so, stay with me. I'll unfold this in a way so that, by the end, you'll clearly get the point that I'm making.

As pianists develop their musicianship, they will often explore different genres. In more "nontraditional" approaches, students will be encouraged to improvise. Improvisation is fundamental to blues and jazz musicians, and one of the most important series of notes that musicians use, when improvising, is known as the "Blues Scale."

For those musicians who have a theoretical understanding, the blues scale is an adaptation of the "Major Scale," and over one octave it consists of the following notes:

The 1 (tonic), 3♭, 4, 5♭, 5, 7♭, and 1.

As I said earlier, if you have no musical background, I don't expect for this to make any sense to you at all. Again, stay with me. If we consider the key of C, let's have a look at what the blues scale looks like when laid out on the piano keyboard:

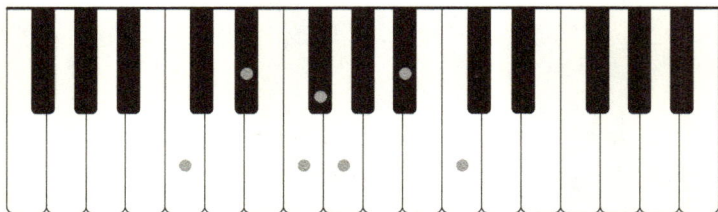

For many, this may still appear like just a random series of dots, but when we join the dots, it draws the shape below, like two broader mountains on either side of a narrow mountain—a very easy visual shape to remember:

EXAMPLE 3: "MOONLIGHT SONATA"

Let's dive into a far more advanced piece of music just to give you an idea of how far reaching this simple, shape-and-pattern-based approach actually can be. We'll use a famous and most beautiful piece of music—the first movement of Beethoven's "Moonlight Sonata."

For the sake of this example, I'll use a section from that piece where the music notation is perhaps the most complex:

When looking at the section highlighted above, and then laying that out onto the keyboard, the entire series of notes ascends then descends its way through a simple, visible pathway across the instrument. It looks like this:

And when we isolate our "constellation," what we're able to clearly see is a wonderfully simple shape that also has a recurring pattern:

To this day, it's delightful for me, when working with advanced musicians and career music-educators who, when presented with these concepts of recognizing shapes and patterns, and who have previously only ever analyzed and translated the notes from the page, exclaim in surprise, "I've been looking at music notation all my life, and these shapes and patterns never occurred to me. Why is it that we aren't teaching this to students from the very beginning?"

Well, in playing-based music education, that's exactly what we do!

"I'm a classically trained violinist and self-taught jazz pianist. When I first spent three days at a Simply Music Teacher Training workshop it was an emotional high. I saw students who had had only eight lessons, play eleven songs from four different genres. The confidence of every student was like nothing I've ever seen. The approach not only makes sense, it makes me wonder why educators ever thought they should teach music in the way that they have, for so long."

—DANE ANDRUS (SIMPLY MUSIC TEACHER)

BEYOND SHAPES AND PATTERNS

Even so, I don't know how common it is for people to hear music in terms of shapes and patterns. All I know is that I've not met very many people for whom that's the case to the same degree as it is for me.

It's also important to understand that Simply Music, as a methodology, goes way beyond merely distilling pieces of music into shapes and patterns. The method, in its entirety, consists of a vast array of playing-based tools and unique learning strategies, including taking into account the five "realms" of learning: generative, receptive, observatory, participatory, and preparatory.

It also places a high emphasis on behavior, and both the dynamics and interplay of the relationship that students and parents have to the process of learning. Having said that, and as I stated earlier in this book, we won't at all be taking a broad-based and in-depth look at Simply Music itself. However, in the next chapter we'll take a somewhat high-level look at more of what the program represents, what it achieves, and how it embodies its mission.

FROM THEN TO NOW

My journey in music education began with codifying the way that music occurred to me as a very young child—through shapes and patterns—it was an organic, unfiltered connection. This wasn't something I created or learned; it was preinstalled, like an app hardwired into my system from birth.

I receive considerable acknowledgment for my work and its impact on people's lives. However, I don't see myself as the creator or source—rather, I view myself as a willing vessel for something that was preordained. My contribution has been the dedication of decades to materializing this perspective into a tangible educational system that many consider a breakthrough. Simply Music emerged not from personal ambition but from a deep sense of purpose and calling.

The notion of Divine Design at play resonates deeply with me, and whether this is "true" or not isn't really my concern. The value that I get is in believing that it's true—and faith always trumps fact.

Through decades of observation and experience, I've come to understand the fundamental limitations of traditional music education—its critical and exclusive nature, and most importantly, its misalignment with what should be its core mission: equipping the population with the ability to be musically self-expressed.

We live in a world rich with music programs and teaching methods, many based on traditional, reading-focused approaches, or emphasizing technical precision and theoretical understanding. While these methods represent well-intentioned attempts to develop advanced musicianship, our current moment in human history calls for something different—a breakthrough that reconnects people with their innate musicality. As beautifully expressed in a quote widely attributed to Rainer Marie Rilke, "The spirit wants only that there be flying. As for who happens to do it, in that he has only a passing interest."

Simply Music emerged as a response to traditional limitations, evolving into a highly structured, scaffolded curriculum that redefines not only who can learn music, but who can successfully teach it. This transformation has led to an international community of educators and students spanning 136 countries, a testament to the hunger for a different approach.

Let's now take a somewhat "high-altitude" look at the Simply Music method as a whole.

"Both our children are learning piano with the Simply Music program, and from the very first day they had smiles of accomplishment from what they could teach me that they had learned. The fact that they learned to play songs long before looking at the music (notation) helped them no end when they did start learning it. The program has helped them naturally to be able to think creatively, and given them incredible memory training and pattern recognition that has helped them with their school also.

The musical start they have been given with your program has made them want to learn other instruments and they both have been told by their cello and violin teachers that they have a good ear and skill for picking up new songs and memory for the tunes, which I 100 percent put down to the Simply Music program. I remember reading Neil Moore's book, *Music and the Art of Long-Term Relationships* soon after they started learning, and it held many truths even in my own life and so when things got stuck, I always referred to this book. I can't thank you enough for creating such a great program. It has brought much joy to our lives."

—HELEN BYRNE (PARENT)

Chapter 7

A NEW METHOD

"I would teach children physics, and philosophy, but most importantly, music, for the patterns in music are the keys to learning."

—PLATO

THE MISSION

Simply Music's mission is to create a breakthrough in access to musical self-expression—to bring musicianship to the masses and, in doing so, help elevate humanity's creative capability. This aligns with what I believe should be the fundamental charter of music education: equipping the population with the ability to be musically self-expressed.

For roughly 300 years, in countries where music has been formally taught, we've attempted to achieve this charter. Yet today, only a tiny percentage of the population can play music. Our prevailing approach to music education has, in important ways, failed its fundamental purpose. To address this failure, we must return to basics and completely rethink our approach.

FIRST-PRINCIPLES THINKING

When tackling any complex problem, we need to start with "first-principles" thinking—examining irreducibly simple, fundamental truths that can't be broken down further. In music education, two such principles stand out with striking clarity.

The first principle is that all human beings, without exception, are profoundly musical. If I could achieve only one thing in my lifetime, it would be bringing this truth into global consciousness. This recognition alone would represent a breakthrough in making musical self-expression accessible to everyone.

The second principle is that the human brain is, by design, a pattern-seeking device. Our brains constantly search for patterns in everything—processes, behavior, structures, shapes—anything we encounter. This isn't just an interesting quirk; it's a fundamental survival mechanism. Your brain's primary purpose is preservation, both immediate and future. Consider how you might sit in your living room, surrounded by familiar sounds and sights, paying attention to none of them—until a new sound immediately grabs your attention because it breaks the pattern. Or how you focus intently when driving a new route, but by the fourth time, you're thinking about dinner—your brain has pattern-mapped the directions, shifting the task from conscious effort to subconscious processing.

When information is presented to the brain in the form of clear, easily recognizable patterns, it's assimilated and processed quickly and effortlessly. In some respects, it's fair to say that pattern-seeking is the brain's playground.

"I started Simply Music to stimulate my aging brain. I'm eighty years old. The effect this program has had on my cognitive function has been extraordinary. I've gone from feeling lazy and being disorganized, to the exact opposite! I am eighty years old, and feel like I'm living proof that learning the piano this way slows the decline of an aging brain. The amount of work and talent that has gone into creating this program is extraordinary."

—VERONICA NICHOLLS (SIMPLY MUSIC STUDENT)

A FOUNDATION FOR LEARNING

Given our first principles—that all humans are inherently musical and that our brains naturally seek patterns—how might we apply these truths to create a music-learning methodology that truly serves the masses? To answer this, I began with a fundamental question: Which is more important—how well people play, or that they can play at all?

When examined through the lens of music education's fundamental charter—equipping the population with musical self-expression—the answer becomes clear. That people play at all must take precedence over how well they play.

Before delving deeper into our approach, it's important to note that Simply Music focuses specifically on piano (or its electronic equivalent). This isn't arbitrary. The piano remains the dominant composition and arranging tool, boasts the largest range of any orchestral instrument, and is a required study for degrees in all other musical instruments. However, while our method unfolds on the piano keyboard, at its core, Simply Music teaches a way of learning. Many of our educators, who teach multiple instruments, report that this method has transformed their approach to teaching across all instruments.

As mentioned in the Introduction, we won't be taking a comprehensive look at Simply Music's inner workings. Instead, we'll explore our underlying philosophy, objectives, and general approach, highlighting key differences between our method and traditional approaches. While we discussed traditional teaching methods in an earlier chapter, revisiting some aspects here will provide valuable context for understanding our alternative approach.

THE READING-BASED TRADITION

In every country where music is formally taught, a single approach dominates: the reading-based method. Billions of dollars are spent annually on music lessons that begin by requiring students to learn how to read music as a means of learning how to play. Even newer teaching methods have largely maintained this traditional starting point.

While generations of students have succeeded with this approach, an exponentially greater number have found that "reading as a means of learning to play" feels unnatural, overly complex, and frustratingly slow. This approach has left too many people believing they're "not musical," that "music isn't for them," that "learning piano is hard," that "you have to start when you're young," that "it takes a long time," or that "you need special talent." As we explored earlier, none of these beliefs hold any truth—they're merely symptoms of our traditional approach's limitations.

DELAYING THE READING OF MUSIC NOTATION

Let me be clear: I wholeheartedly believe in the value of learning to read music. Being unable to do so would be like speaking your native language fluently but remaining illiterate—an extremely limiting condition. However, the critical question isn't whether students should learn to read music, but when and how this skill should be developed.

One fundamental difference between Simply Music and traditional reading-based programs is our deliberate delay of the reading process until after students have established a comprehensive playing repertoire. The rationale mirrors natural language acquisition: Children are born into an environment where language surrounds them. Parents model language simply by speaking, and children naturally absorb and replicate it. Just as our species has a neurological propensity for language, we have an innate capacity for musicality. We're all inherently musical, just as we're all inherently verbal.

I believe that requiring beginning students to first learn music notation before playing isn't just counterproductive—it's preposterous. This requirement has been one of the primary barriers preventing countless students from connecting with their natural musicianship.

Consider this: We would never require children to learn reading and spelling as a prerequisite for speaking! Why, then, do we insist that students must read music before they can play? In reality, we all spoke fluently for years before learning to read and write. If we truly accept music as a universal language—which it absolutely is—we must treat it with the same respect and understanding we give to verbal language acquisition.

"After a year of traditional lessons our son was only playing one hand and one note at a time. He was discouraged and ready to quit. We then switched him to Simply Music and he now plays blues, jazz and classical pieces. He *loves* piano now."

—REBECCA BOLIN (PARENT)

THE TECHNIQUE-BASED TRADITION

Traditional music education places an extraordinarily high premium on technical precision—the physical aspects of advanced performance. Most formally trained music educators emphasize rigorous attention to posture, hand positioning, hand shaping, intonation, fingering, and physical execution. This technical focus typically requires teachers to possess extensive training and high-level playing abilities themselves.

In this environment, students must dedicate significant practice time to scales, drills, and exercises—with particular emphasis on finger strengthening and finger independence. While this technical rigor is well-intentioned, and perhaps necessary for those pursuing advanced classical performance, it creates barriers for the vast majority of students. For them, music learning becomes overly rigid and demanding, sacrificing musical variety and natural self-expression. The simple joy of playing great-sounding pieces gets lost in the pursuit of technical perfection.

DISCOVERING TECHNIQUE

Consider again the parallel with spoken language. Parents don't formally train their children in the complex techniques of speech—the intricate interplay of hard and soft palate, tongue positioning, lip shaping, vocal cord activation, and diaphragm control. Instead, we acquire speech through osmosis—discovering and refining these skills through direct experience rather than formal instruction. We learn by doing, on the field of action, rather than through technical explanation.

Students who simply want music as an everyday companion, who seek the pure enjoyment of playing a repertoire of great-sounding pieces, need an approach that transforms the speed and ease of learning. This doesn't mean technique is unimportant—an appropriate technical foundation, relevant to each student's aspirations, remains valuable as musical maturity develops. However, for the vast majority who want to experience music as a joyful pastime, technique can be discovered naturally through the learning process.

The key is folding technique into the learning journey in a more organic way, similar to how we learn many daily activities. Think about typing on digital devices, tying shoelaces, brushing teeth, fastening buttons, threading needles, or driving cars—we master these skills through direct experience and discovery. Musical technique can be developed in the same natural, experiential way.

"For nine years I taught a method which was faster and simpler than the traditional approach, but the Simply Music program has blown even that out of the water. I dream of a world where everyone plays music and experiences the pure joy of musical self-expression! The Simply Music program, more so than anything I've ever seen or taught before, takes that vision from being just a possibility and begins to make it a reality. I am moved, excited, and inspired to be part of a team of people who will actually be causing those kinds of changes in the world. The program is genius in its simplicity."

—KERRY HALBERT (SIMPLY MUSIC TEACHER)

THE THEORY-BASED TRADITION

Traditional music education places significant emphasis on music theory—the mathematical and structural elements of music. Students are required to master scales, key signatures, modes, chord construction, and progressions. While the science of music is undeniably fascinating for those who are drawn to it, requiring theoretical understanding from students who simply want music in their lives often creates unnecessary complications and barriers.

Once again, the language parallel proves illuminating. We don't begin teaching speech with grammar theory—conjugating verbs, differentiating nouns from pronouns, or analyzing past participles. Just because something can be explained mathematically doesn't mean it should be.

The traditional approach creates a triple burden: Students must simultaneously process complex notation translation, master precise technical requirements, and understand theoretical concepts. This multilayered demand directly conflicts with our neurological reality—the human brain is designed for single-thought processing. For most students, this combination of reading, technique, and theory creates an overwhelming learning environment. This helps explain why, after 300 years of formal music education, only a fraction of the population can play music.

INTEGRATED THEORY

A more effective approach emerges when we first establish a foundation of playing ability, then introduce theoretical concepts as they become relevant to what students can already play. Theory takes on an enlightening quality when it directly enhances the student's enjoyment and understanding of music they've already mastered. This parallels how we naturally deepen our understanding of any skill—through experience first, followed by comprehension of the underlying principles.

Consider again our relationship with spoken language: The vast majority of people navigate complex verbal communication daily without any conscious awareness of the theoretical framework that underlies their speech. This raises crucial questions about the timing and necessity of theoretical instruction in music education. When does theoretical understanding become truly necessary? Why is it needed at any particular point in the learning journey?

Moreover, we must consider the neurological implications. Theoretical explanations engage entirely different neural pathways than the direct playing experience. Are we inadvertently creating barriers to natural musical development by emphasizing theoretical understanding too early? Just as we allow language skills to develop organically before introducing grammar rules, perhaps we should let musical fluency establish itself before overlaying theoretical frameworks.

Let me be clear: Traditional music education has undeniably produced outstanding musicians and brilliant educators. We owe much to this system that's preserved and perpetuated the works of great composers like Chopin, Beethoven, Mozart, and Bach. Their contributions continue to enrich our cultural heritage.

However, we're now far from traditional times. Never before in human history has there been such an urgent need to integrate musicianship into our daily experience. The time has come to usher in a new era of music education—one that aligns with both our fundamental charter and our first principles. We need an approach that opens the door to musical expression for everyone, not just the technically gifted few.

"I had years of classical experience, but Simply Music music gave me a whole new color palette to play with. I started feeling more freedom, to know what to do, to create my own arrangements, to take a chord sheet and be able to fill in gaps. I was able to scaffold my own learning."

—LISA BLASI (SIMPLY MUSIC TEACHER)

PLAYING-BASED LEARNING: A NEW APPROACH

The Simply Music method creates a new category in learn-ing—playing-based music education. This approach immerses students in the actual process of playing, using real pieces as the arena for unfolding and developing the subtleties of musical expression.

Think about how we learn life's essential skills: tying shoe-laces, brushing teeth, buttoning shirts—all through direct experience, not by studying theory or referring to notes. We learn by doing. Similarly, playing-based learning draws on stu-dents' existing visual, aural, and physical skills, combining these with their natural sense of musicality.

From the very first lessons, we translate pieces of music into a unique series of simple, playing-based concepts. This neurolog-ically aligned approach has students recognizing and visualizing shapes and patterns as they unfold directly onto the keyboard. Freed from the immediate burden of reading music, students develop a deep and personal relationship with the instrument.

Within this song-centered focus, technical projects and the-oretical concepts are subtly woven into the total experience over time. Through extensive experience, we've found that develop-mentally appropriate technique emerges most naturally and effectively when introduced this way. The technical skills and theoretical understanding that best serve players who want to express themselves in the broadest possible way are those acquired in harmony with how our body and brain naturally work. This approach proves surprisingly transparent, compar-atively simple, and highly enjoyable.

From their very first lessons, students are playing quality pieces, from beginning to end, using both hands, and across a range of styles including contemporary, classical, ballads, and blues. The experience is tactile and multisensory, engaging students physically, visually, and aurally. After building a repertoire of forty to fifty pieces—typically within the first twelve to eighteen months—students begin learning our unique approach to reading music.

This approach naturally dovetails with the practical, playing-based skills they've already acquired. Most importantly, their established playing ability provides a powerful foundation for learning the more formal aspects of music education. Throughout their journey, Simply Music students are gently encouraged to explore their natural self-expression through arrangements, accompaniment, improvisation, and composition. We consider all these elements essential components of a comprehensive, broad-based music education.

"Speaking as a professional composer, I'm impressed with the way the Simply Music program has been constructed. My nine-year-old son is not only playing the songs in the Simply Music repertory, he's improvising his own tunes, reading chord changes, and teaching himself new songs. That's really worth its weight in gold."

—JAMES DI PASQUALE, (PARENT, PROFESSIONAL FILM COMPOSER AND JAZZ MUSICIAN)

DR. ROSALIE CLARK'S ANALYSIS

Dr. Clark holds a doctorate of philosophy and a bachelor of social science (honours) from the University of KwaZulu-Natal, South Africa; a master of education from Macquarie University, Australia; and a bachelor of theology from Charles Sturt University, Australia. When she conducted an educational analysis of Simply Music, her insights were powerful. After studying our program for several years, she wrote:

> Simply Music as a music teaching method is exceptional in its ability to "scaffold" learning experiences for music students. By doing this, it maximizes the co-constructivist theory of education that asserts that a teacher's role is to coach, model, and support students as they learn new concepts. The teacher then allows students to take on this acquired knowledge and embrace it as their own. This approach to education builds on the work of educational theorist, Vygotsky, and his idea of moving students into their "zone of proximal development.

> As a teaching method, Simply Music does this by being carefully structured, especially in its reference to ensuring students are always using 'single thought processes' to assimilate new information. As a method, Simply Music is always striving to have students become conscious of the learning tools that are behind the learning so that students are "learning a new way of learning" and not just being filled with content.

> The co-constructivist approach to education is a socio-cultural approach to learning which asserts that a student's success in learning depends largely on the appropriate role, instruction, and support from significant others in a student's life. As a method, Simply Music supports this approach by encouraging strong parental support in lessons and at home, as well as careful attention paid by teachers to students in individual or shared lessons.

> Perhaps the most significant attribute of this method is that by holding firmly the values behind a co-constructivist theoretical

approach to teaching, it allows the music student to be transformed by his/her music education. This transformation does not occur because he/she has been filled with knowledge. It occurs because through being a collaborative participant in their learning, students have been given skills to express their natural musical ability on the piano.

Simply Music is in a unique position to take more modern theoretical approaches to education into the music education arena. It's in a unique position because it has such a track record of success in student and teacher growth and participation, as well as being far ahead and well developed in curriculum resources.[17]

"As a result of a spontaneous cerebral hemorrhage, I sustained a serious brain injury and was no longer engaged in gainful employment. With the help of my care-provider, we found Simply Music. It has been of fantastic benefit to me, in that it enabled me to play the piano immediately. It is a superior method of learning in that it encourages the brain to forge new (and old) pathways, enhancing healing! In short, I've found the Simply Music program to be of enormous benefit to me in my rehabilitation. It's the glue that is bringing my brain back together."

—TERESA KILLEEN (SIMPLY MUSIC STUDENT)

---

17   Dr. Rosalie Clark, letter of analysis regarding Simply Music, Perth, Australia, July 2004.

OUR GOALS AND VISION

Simply Music aims for students to acquire and retain music as a lifelong companion. This overarching mission breaks down into four specific goals:

- Playing a huge repertoire across genres and styles
- Experiencing playing as natural self-expression
- Enjoying music as a highly positive, self-affirming pursuit
- Developing the ability to self-generate, i.e., to be able to progress independently

THE RELATIONSHIP CONVERSATION

For music to become a lifelong companion, an alignment of objectives among students, parents, and educators is essential. Simply Music not only introduces a new methodology but examines the behavioral aspects of learning through a fresh lens. This manifests directly in the lesson environment, where students and parents discover a new understanding of what's required to build a lifelong relationship with music.

We call this ongoing dialogue "The Relationship Conversation," and this conversation is elaborated on in my book, *Music and the Art of Long-Term Relationships*. At its core, the framework of this conversation redefines our approach to music education; supports fostering a deep, lifelong connection with music; and, perhaps most importantly, develops skills for navigating any long-term relationship in life.

The essence of the Relationship Conversation lies in an understanding of the natural rhythm of peaks, plateaus, and valleys that characterizes any enduring engagement. In addition, it provides a model of interpretation that provides a powerful and effective way to relate to these phases.

The Relationship Conversation reveals a profound truth: The skills developed in navigating music education's peaks, plateaus, and valleys transfer directly to all aspects of life. Through understanding and accepting these natural phases as necessary steps in growth, students develop patience, persistence, and deeper empathy—qualities that serve them in personal connections, professional pursuits, and other passions. What begins as a framework for musical development transcends its original purpose, demonstrating music's extraordinary power as a medium for lifelong learning. This understanding fosters not just musical self-expression, but cultivates the resilience and wisdom needed to navigate life's complexities, ultimately leading to a richer, more connected existence. In this way, the journey of musical learning becomes a masterclass in building and sustaining meaningful relationships of all kinds.

CHANGING LIVES, BUILDING FUTURES

When all is said and done, what matters most is this fundamental truth: All human beings are profoundly musical, and we now have a methodology that aligns with how the brain naturally learns. Students can immediately connect with their musicianship, experiencing the absolute fun and sheer pleasure of musical self-expression, while simultaneously providing their brains with critical neurological nutrition. This engagement builds neural connectivity, develops creative capability, and helps future-proof cognitive health—all through an activity that's deeply engaging and fundamentally human.

Over decades, I've witnessed the profound impact of playing-based learning. Adults in their sixties, seventies, and eighties who've spent lifetimes yearning to play music finally experience their natural musicianship. When they begin playing in their very first lessons, tears often flow—not just from joy, but from the release of a lifetime's burden of believing they lacked musical ability.

This methodology has transformed lives across the globe. From typical learners to those with significant learning differences, from individuals with special needs to those carrying previous musical trauma, all have discovered a new pathway to self-expression. In doing so, they're not just enriching their own lives—they're developing the creative capabilities that humanity desperately needs for the unprecedented changes ahead.

"Savannah is nine years old. Simply Music has been great for her fundamental core building and belief in herself. She is so used to other people quitting on her, whereas the consistency and continuity of this program has had a profound effect on her. Weekly lessons are a highlight for her, with weekly accomplishments building self-belief and self-esteem. Savannah is now able to express herself musically and loves to make musical sense on the keyboard. The reward of hearing the results of her efforts is instrumental in developing her concentration, confidence, patience, endurance and perseverance. It has broadened her world."

—GISELLE ROZNICKI, PARENT OF SAVANNAH (WHO HAS AUTISM)

LOOKING FORWARD

As we stand at the threshold of transformative technological and social change, imagine a world where playing-based music education has achieved mass adoption. What might society look like if the majority of people had access to their natural musicality? How might this shift in creative capability reshape our collective future?

In the next chapter, we'll explore this vision—a future where musical self-expression is truly democratized, where creative thinking is the norm rather than the exception, and where humanity's innate musicality serves as a crucial resource for navigating the challenges and opportunities that lie ahead. The groundwork has been laid; the methodology exists.

Let's imagine how this transformation—a new era of music education, a new possibility for humanity—may have reshaped our world.

Chapter 8

A WORLD WHERE EVERYONE PLAYS

"Music gives a soul to the universe, wings to the mind, flight to the imagination, and life to everything."

—PLATO

FROM TRADITIONAL TIMES TO TOMORROW

Let's pause for a moment to reiterate something important: Traditional music education, despite its complexities, has contributed greatly to society. It preserved great works, developed extraordinary musicians and educators, and brought us much of the rich musical world we cherish today. However, we're now right on the cusp of unprecedented technological change. What's needed isn't merely an improvement on something from the past, but a completely new approach to music education that's accessible to humanity as a whole—it's time for the era of "music for the masses."

In the spirit of visionary thinking and creative expression, let's imagine a possible reality, and one that could well be in a not-too-distant future. Let's stand in that future and look back on what happened as a result of the mass proliferation of playing-based music education and the impact it had throughout the world.

THE TRANSFORMATION UNFOLDS

Just as we came to understand the necessity of nutritional supplements in an era where modern agriculture had depleted our food's nutritional density, and just like the widespread adoption of practices such as meditation and yoga for mental and physical well-being, musicianship became understood as fundamental to cognitive health and creative development. As our world demanded new levels of adaptability, and new solutions to unprecedented challenges, this understanding saw the reprioritization of music-education moving from social pleasure and its academic interest to practical necessity. Creative capability emerged as the dominant personal attribute necessary for flourishing in the new future.

Science-based research continued to reveal more and more about the positive impact that musicianship could have at neurological, psychological, and emotional levels, and the outcome of this research contributed significantly to accelerating the widespread adoption of playing-based learning.

What emerged wasn't just a new approach to music education—it was a fundamental shift in how society prioritized the role of music. Music education shifted from performance excellence to personal development, from technical exactness to creative expression. It was truly about recognizing music as a language, and authentically treating it as such.

Playing-based music education became transformational

in democratizing and culturally redefining who was capable of successfully teaching music. This led to the emergence of a vast and entirely new generation of music educators and facilitators—from advanced and formally trained musicians to comparative beginners and enthusiasts—who discovered that they had the ability, and methodology, that would allow them to share entry-level music education at an unprecedented level.

This wasn't a matter of aiming to turn everyone into advanced, concert-level, professional musicians. Rather, it was about providing everyone access to an activity that provided enormous emotional, psychological, and social benefits, while also developing the neural connectivity essential for "new thinking" in the "new future."

HEALTHCARE

Drug and alcohol rehabilitation centers incorporated music learning into their recovery programs, discovering its positive impact on healing and neural regeneration. Hospitals discovered that patients who engaged in music learning during recovery showed accelerated healing rates. Veterans facilities found that music education offered new pathways for processing trauma, rebuilding neural pathways, and enhancing self-confidence, self-expression, self-worth, and self-esteem. Mental health professionals found that music learning provided a unique form of cognitive therapy. Memory care facilities reported that residents who participated in music learning maintained, even regained, stronger cognitive function. Women's shelters discovered that learning music provided not just emotional solace but enhanced cognitive resilience—exactly what their residents needed to rebuild their lives. And of major importance, medical insurance began covering music learning as both preparatory and preventive care for emotional, psychological, and cognitive health.

EDUCATION

Educational institutions recognized that music learning wasn't competing with STEM subjects—it was enhancing students' capability to master them. Schools shifted from treating music as an "extra" to recognizing it as a core curriculum. Instead of teaching music to create musicians, they used playing-based music education to also develop creative thinkers. The results were powerful: students showed enhanced problem-solving abilities across all subjects. More importantly, they developed the neural flexibility needed to adapt to rapid change.

PROFESSIONAL DEVELOPMENT

Businesses began incorporating music learning into their innovation programs. Corporate wellness programs included music education alongside fitness benefits. Companies that incorporated music learning into their innovation programs saw increases in creative problem-solving. Teams that learned and played music together showed improved collaboration skills. The pattern-recognition abilities developed through music learning transferred directly to market analysis and strategic planning.

THE SOCIAL IMPACT

Communities began to change. Senior centers became hubs of cognitive vitality, where elders who engaged in music learning maintained sharper minds well into their later years. Retirement communities found that residents who engaged in music learning maintained cognitive flexibility far longer than those who didn't. Community centers offered playing-based music education as a standard service, recognizing its role in developing local creative capability. The focus shifted from creating performers to nurturing creative potential.

Perhaps most significantly, this "music for the masses" transformation helped bridge the growing divide between technology and human experience. As advancements transformed traditional roles, and began to redefine life on Earth, people focused on developing their uniquely human capabilities. Music learning became a pathway to enhance creative thinking and help integrate human intelligence and expression into the new future.

THE PERSONAL REVOLUTION

What made this broader, societal transformation so powerful was its deeply personal impact. People discovered that fifteen to twenty minutes of music practice, done merely several times a week, was impacting their cognitive capability. Adults who had always believed they "weren't musical" found themselves playing enjoyable pieces within weeks, and discovering a new and wonderful form of self-expression. More importantly, they noticed changes in how they approached problems in their daily lives—seeing patterns they hadn't noticed before, finding creative solutions more readily.

Children growing up in this new paradigm never developed the limiting beliefs that had held back previous generations. They experienced music as naturally as language, and with it, were developing the neurological machinery needed for an increasingly complex world. The question was no longer

"Are you musical?" but rather "How are you using music to develop your creative capability, and how are you expressing your creativity?"

THE FUTURE UNFOLDED

Looking back, it seems almost obvious: Just as we saw the need for physical exercise to maintain our bodies, and meditation to calm our minds, we saw that we needed the critical neurological nutrition of musicianship to future-prepare our minds. The playing-based revolution wasn't about merely replacing traditional music education; it was about democratizing music learning, making it as accessible and normal as spoken language.

A NEW UNDERSTANDING

Now, as we are back in present time, standing here and looking ahead into the extraordinary unpredictability of whatever is to come, one thing is certain—the one personal attribute that will dominate and lead the future will be creativity. The future will belong to those who can think creatively, adapt readily, and maintain their essential humanity while embracing transformation. Playing-based music education provides a proven pathway to developing these capabilities. It's not just about preserving our musical heritage anymore—it's about preparing humanity for whatever challenges lie ahead.

As we extend our reach to Mars and beyond, we carry with us this profound understanding: Our most powerful tool for future adaptation isn't just technological advancement—it's the development of our uniquely human capabilities. Music—that ancient practice we discovered millennia ago—turns out to be exactly what we need to thrive in the future we're creating.

This is the New Case for Creativity, the new case for playing-based music education: not merely as entertainment or cultural enrichment, but as essential preparation for human flourishing in an era of unprecedented change. The question isn't whether we should make music learning universally accessible—it's how quickly we can implement this transformation. Our future will depend on it.

CONCLUSION

"Creativity now is as important in education as literacy."

—SIR KEN ROBINSON

Throughout this book, we've embarked on a profound journey, exploring the unprecedented technological changes that lie ahead, the crucial role of creative capability in navigating this new future, and the transformative power of playing-based music education in helping to develop this capability.

As we stand at the precipice of a future that will redefine not just how we live but what it means to be human, one truth emerges with striking clarity: Our success, both individually and collectively, will hinge on our ability to think creatively, adapt readily, and maintain our essential humanity while embracing transformation. In this context, playing-based music education emerges not as a mere nicety but as an essential—a proven pathway to developing the neural connectivity that underlies creative thinking and problem-solving.

The case for prioritizing music learning has never been stronger. Science has shown us that engaging in music learning can impact brain development and neural connectivity in a unique way—more than twice as much as sports and other forms of art. History has demonstrated music's integral role in human evolution and expression. And now, as we face a future of unparalleled change, music offers us a powerful tool to develop the potential we will need to not just survive but thrive.

But to fully harness this potential, we must fundamentally rethink our approach to music education. The traditional model, with its emphasis on reading, technique, theory, and rigid standards of performance, has served an important purpose but has also created barriers to widespread musical engagement. It's time for a new era—one that recognizes the universality of human musicality, aligns with the brain's natural learning processes, and prioritizes musical experience and creative expression over technical perfection.

This is the promise and the imperative of playing-based music education. By immersing students in the actual experience of playing from their very first lessons, this approach taps into our innate musicality, builds neural connectivity, and develops creative capability—all while fostering a lifelong love for musical expression. It's a model that can be applied across ages, abilities, and aspirations, offering a pathway to personal growth and cognitive development for all.

The implications extend far beyond the realm of music. The technological transformations on the horizon will impact every facet of our lives—from our careers and financial situations to our relationships and sense of purpose. In the face of such profound change, it's easy to feel overwhelmed, helpless, even highly resistant. But herein lies the beauty of music: It offers us a simple, profoundly human way to develop the very capabilities we'll need most.

By investing just a few minutes each day in learning to play music, we're not just enriching our lives with the sheer fun and beautiful form of self-expression that it is—we're actually rewiring our brains for enhanced adaptability, resilience, and creative expression. We're giving ourselves a powerful tool to navigate the challenges and opportunities ahead, and to find meaning and purpose in a world that's rapidly changing.

The bottom line is simple. This is a call to action—for individuals, educators, policymakers, and society as a whole. It's time to recognize the transformative power of musicianship—learning to play—and to make it a priority in our homes, our schools, and our communities. The stakes couldn't be higher, but the path forward is clear.

By embracing music as a tool for developing our creative capability, we're not just investing in our individual potential—we're investing in the future of our species. We're equipping ourselves, and our children, with the skills to navigate an uncertain world, to find solutions to problems we can't yet imagine, and to create a future that's not just technologically advanced, but deeply, beautifully human.

The journey ahead will be challenging, but it's also filled with incredible possibility. As we stand on the threshold of this new era, we need to become fully conscious of the power that lies within us—the power of our innate musicality, of our boundless creativity, of our extraordinary resilience and adaptability.

The future is uncertain, but our creativity isn't. Let's harness it, nurture it, and use it to build a future worthy of our highest aspirations. The journey begins now, and it begins with the simple, profound act of making music.

This is the real "Music on Mars"—the music of a species that's harnessed its innate capabilities to create a future of possibility. It's a future where creativity and vision-in-action aren't the domain of a gifted few but the birthright of every human being. A future where we face the unknown not with fear and resistance, but with the confidence that comes from knowing we have the tools to adapt, innovate, and thrive.

ACKNOWLEDGEMENTS

First and foremost, my deepest love and gratitude goes to my extraordinary wife, and angel-on-earth, Hunter. Having met when she was just twelve and I was thirteen, we recently celebrated fifty-four years of friendship and forty-three years of marriage at the time of this writing. Her unwavering support, not just through the writing of this book but through the entire journey of creating Simply Music and navigating life's complexities, has been a constant source of strength. She has profoundly fueled my appreciation for the life I have and the life we've built together.

I also extend my love and heartfelt thanks to my three wonderful children, Leon, Chase, and Remy. Their patience, understanding, and support, even in the face of decisions that have significantly impacted their lives, have been truly humbling. Although both of my parents passed before the publication of this book, I am forever grateful for the beautiful lives they modeled, the life they gave me, and their nurturing of my musical gift. I also extend my thanks to my four older siblings, particularly my sister, Anne, and my brother Gary, whose friendship, love and counsel I value.

I am deeply grateful to Igor Zambelli, my best friend of many decades, a tireless supporter, and a patron of Simply Music. My thanks also to Mary K Ferreter for her friendship, relentless loyalty, support and love. I also extend, posthumously, my love, appreciation and gratitude to Gordon Harvey, whose decades of friendship, and contribution to Simply Music, were both extraordinary and profound.

Endless thanks to my incredible team at Simply Music, the hundreds of Simply Music educators worldwide, and the many tens of thousands of Simply Music students who are the living embodiment of my methodology. Their dedication and passion are the ultimate validation of the power of playing-based music education and its role in shaping humanity's future. A special thanks to Stacie Davison, Laurie Richards, Robin Quinn Keehn, Bernadette Ashby, Stephanie Iadanza, Mark Meritt and Kerry Hanley. They each have been relentless in their support of me, the vision I hold for Simply Music, and their stand for the possibility of a world where everyone plays.

I'm deeply grateful to the founders of the entrepreneurial communities I am privileged to be a part of—Joe Polish, Peter Diamandis, Giovanni Marsico, Steve Sims, and Dan Sullivan—I thank each of them for their friendship and mentorship over the years. My thanks also to Simply Music patron, Ron Mannix, whose encouragement, belief in Simply Music, and generous support are deeply appreciated.

Writing a book, much like learning to play music, isn't a solo endeavor. It's a symphony of support, encouragement, and shared belief. To everyone who's been a part of this symphony, whether by contributing directly to the book or by enriching my life with your presence: Thank you, from the depths of my heart.

May this book be not just a culmination, but a beginning— the start of a new movement in how we understand and embrace the transformative power of music. And may that movement, like the music that inspires it, resonate far beyond these pages.

APPENDIX

NEUROLOGICAL RESEARCH

The scientific exploration of the benefits of music education has significantly increased in recent decades, particularly in the realm of its neuroscience. The relationship between music and the brain suggests a profound correlation between music learning and enhanced neural connectivity. This connection establishes a foundation for an array of cognitive benefits and improved creative capability, along with indicating an array of physical, emotional, and behavioral benefits.

The heart of the human brain's functionality lies in its network of neurons connected to and transmitting information through synapses. The efficiency and strength of these connections are imperative for cognitive function, memory, and learning. Music education augments the strength of these neural connections.

Studies such as those by Hyde et al. demonstrate that children engaged in music-learning exhibit enhanced structural connectivity between regions crucial for auditory and motor tasks, which not only refines their music performance but also lays a strong foundation for learning across other domains.[18]

Moreover, music learning has been associated with an increase in gray matter volume, particularly in areas related to auditory processing and motor control.[19] This growth suggests a potential edge for music students and performers in these domains over those who haven't had music education. The benefits of music learning extend to the brain's white matter as well, which facilitates communication between various parts of the brain. Engaging in musical activities has shown to enhance the structure of white matter tracts, and as a result, potentially translating to quicker thinking, improved memory, and better problem-solving abilities.[20]

The ripple effect of enhanced neural connectivity through music education extends to creative neurology. Creative capability, often visualized as the brain's ability to connect disparate ideas in novel ways, requires the seamless integration of various brain regions. The rich array of patterns, rhythms, melodies, and harmonies in music challenges the brain to form connections that might not typically be engaged together.

This engagement with musical patterns and, in particular, music improvisation can foster increased innovative thought and out-of-the-box problem-solving, thereby nurturing a breeding ground for creative capability through heightened brain plasticity.

18 Krista L. Hyde et al., "Musical Training Shapes Structural Brain Development," *Journal of Neuroscience* 29, no. 10 (March 11, 2009): 3019–25, https://doi.org/10.1523/jneurosci.5118-08.2009.

19 Christian Gaser and Gottfried Schlaug, "Brain Structures Differ Between Musicians and Non-Musicians," *Journal of Neuroscience* 23, no. 27 (October 8, 2003): 9240–25, https://doi.org/10.1523/jneurosci.23-27-09240.2003.

20 Gus F. Halwani et al., "Effects of Practice and Experience on the Arcuate Fasciculus: Comparing Singers, Instrumentalists, and Non-Musicians," *Frontiers in Psychology* 2 (July 6, 2011): 156, https://doi.org/10.3389/fpsyg.2011.00156.

Furthermore, the direct impact of neural connectivity on creative capability is significant. The more interconnected our neural networks are, the richer and more diverse our creative outputs can become. Enhanced connectivity allows for faster and more efficient communication between different brain regions, which is essential for the merging of unrelated ideas, a cornerstone of creative thinking.

Beyond the neurological and creative realms, music education offers numerous benefits across physical, emotional, and behavioral dimensions—from improved fine motor skills, enhanced respiratory control, and better cardiovascular health to stress reduction, increased self-esteem, emotional resilience, increased neural connectivity, and the development of creative capabilities. Additionally, behavioral advantages such as enhanced concentration, improved discipline, and teamwork are notable.

The journey from the prenatal stage to elderhood presents a series of developmental milestones. In this next section, we delve deeper into exploring how these neurological, creative, and holistic benefits manifest across various life stages. Let's briefly explore the impact of music education at each of these pivotal life stages.

IMPACT ON PRENATAL DEVELOPMENT

The prenatal period is a critical time for the development of the auditory system and overall neural development in fetuses. Around the twentieth week of gestation, a fetus begins to hear sounds from the outside world, and introducing music to the unborn baby during this time has been suggested to provide stimulation to their developing brain. This stimulation aids in the auditory development of the fetus and may establish early patterns of cognition and emotion.

A study by Partanen et al. supports this notion as it found that fetuses can recognize and remember sounds from the outside world, which indicates an impact on early neural development.[21] Furthermore, music intervention during the prenatal period has shown to have significant benefits on the fetus. A study monitored the fetal heart rate and movement responses to familiar and unfamiliar music in pregnant women between thirty and thirty-eight weeks of gestational age. The results revealed that unborn babies who were exposed to music while in the womb showed a significant improvement in their overall mental, cognitive, behavioral, sensory, psychological, and emotional development compared to those who were not exposed to music.[22]

Another study observed that fetuses who had listened to a particular piece of music during previous sessions significantly increased their heart rate accelerations and movements during the music listening session of the last nonstress test, although no significant changes were observed in the number of uterine contractions.[23]

Additionally, it's suggested that prenatal sound stimulation, including music and speech, can form stimulus-specific memory traces during the fetal period, which may affect the neonatal neural system. However, further research with

---

21 Eino Partanen et al., "Learning-Induced Neural Plasticity of Speech Processing Before Birth," *Proceedings of the National Academy of Sciences* 110, no. 37 (August 26, 2013): 15145–50, https://doi.org/10.1073/pnas.1302159110.

22 Liza Lee et al., "The Effect of Music Intervention on Fetal Education via Doppler Fetal Monitor," *Children* 9, no. 6 (2022): 918, https://doi.org/10.3390/children9060918.

23 Eleonora Brillo et al., "The Effect of Prenatal Exposure to Music on Fetal Movements and Fetal Heart Rate: A Pilot Study," *Journal of Maternal-Fetal & Neonatal Medicine* 34, no. 14 (2021): 2274–82, https://doi.org/10.1080/14767058.2019.1663817.

precisely designed methodologies is needed to validate and understand these effects comprehensively.[24]

Moreover, music is considered a noninvasive and culturally acceptable intervention with multiple potential direct and indirect beneficial effects on both the mother and fetus throughout the pregnancy and perinatal period. In animals, prenatal music exposure has been shown to improve postnatal spatial learning and memory, as well as reduce isolation stress.[25]

Lastly, extensive prenatal exposure to a melody has been shown to induce neural representations that last for several months, suggesting that rather than being born as a "blank slate," a newborn has surprisingly extensive experiences of the surrounding world, which are shaped in part by prenatal auditory experiences like music exposure.[26]

IMPACT ON INFANCY AND EARLY CHILDHOOD (ZERO TO FIVE YEARS OLD)

The profound influence of music on human emotions and cognition has been recognized since ancient times. The modern era has brought a plethora of research underscoring the multifaceted impact of music and music education on child development, from infancy through early childhood. Engaging with music, whether it be through listening, singing, or playing instruments, fosters a rich environment for brain development, creativity nurturing, and emotional, psychological, and behav-

24   Kobra Movalled et al., "The Impact of Sound Simulations During Pregnancy on Fetal Learning: A Systematic Review," *BMC Pediatrics* 23 (2023): 183, https://doi.org/10.1186/s12887-023-03990-7.

25   Ravindra Arya et al., "Maternal Music Exposure During Pregnancy Influences Neonatal Behaviour: An Open-Label Randomized Controlled Trial," *International Journal of Pediatrics* 2012, no. 1 (January 2012): 901812, https://doi.org/10.1155/2012/901812.

26   Partanen et al., "Prenatal Music Exposure."

ioral growth. Music education significantly contributes to early childhood development in a variety of areas.

COGNITIVE DEVELOPMENT

- **Enhanced Auditory Discrimination:** Early exposure to music can help infants distinguish between different types of sounds, which is foundational for language development.[27]
- **Spatial Reasoning:** Music can aid in developing spatial-temporal reasoning skills, essential for understanding mathematics and science concepts later in life.[28]
- **Boosted Memory Skills:** Simple song repetitions can enhance short-term and long-term recall in infants.[29]
- **Enhanced Neural Plasticity:** Music education has been found to enhance neural plasticity, the brain's ability to change and adapt as a result of experience. Early music learning develops a larger neural network with more synchronized communication between different brain regions. This is especially significant in early childhood when the brain is most plastic and receptive to learning.[30]
- **Strengthened Executive Function:** Music education also bolsters executive functions, which include working memory, attention control, and cognitive flexibility. Studies

27 Laurel J. Trainor and Becky M. Heinmiller, "The Development of Evaluative Responses to Music: Infants Prefer to Listen to Consonance Over Dissonance," *Infant Behavior and Development* 21, no. 1 (1998): 77–88, https://doi.org/10.1016/S0163-6383(98)90055-8.

28 Frances H. Rauscher and Sean C. Hinton, "Music Instruction and Its Diverse Extra-Musical Benefits," *Music Perception* 29, no. 2 (2011): 215–26, https://doi.org/10.1525/mp.2011.29.2.215.

29 Jayne M. Standley and Jane E. Hughes, "Evaluation of an Early Intervention Music Curriculum for Enhancing Prereading/Writing Skills," *Music Therapy Perspectives* 15, no. 2 (1997): 79–86, https://doi.org/10.1093/mtp/15.2.79.

30 Gottfried Schlaug et al., "Effects of Music Training on the Child's Brain and Cognitive Development," *Annals of the New York Academy of Sciences* 1060, no. 1 (December 2005): 219–30, https://doi.org/10.1196/annals.1360.015.

show that children with music learning exhibit better verbal memory, spatial reasoning, and literacy skills.[31]

SOCIAL AND EMOTIONAL DEVELOPMENT

- **Increased Bonding:** Singing and rhythmic activities promote bonding between the child and caregiver, enhancing the attachment process.[32]
- **Social Skills:** Group musical activities, like group singing or circle time with instruments, can foster social interaction and cooperation among toddlers.[33]
- **Emotion Recognition:** Music education helps children in recognizing and expressing their emotions. It also fosters empathy by helping children understand the emotions conveyed in music. Even infants can recognize basic emotions in music, such as happiness in a major key or sadness in a minor key.[34]
- **Self-Regulation:** Listening to lullabies or calming music can help infants and toddlers learn to soothe themselves, an essential skill for emotional regulation.[35]

31   B. Hanna-Pladdy and A. Mackay, "The Relation Between Instrumental Musical Activity and Cognitive Aging," *Neuropsychology* 25, no. 3 (2011): 378–86, https://psycnet.apa.org/doi/10.1037/a0021895.

32   Sandra E. Trehub and Laurel Trainor, "Singing to Infants: Lullabies and Play Songs," *Advances in Infancy Research* 12 (1998): 43–78, https://trainorlab.mcmaster.ca/publications/pdfs/trainor_trehub.pdf.

33   David Gerry et al., "Active Music Classes in Infancy Enhance Musical, Communicative and Social Development," *Developmental Science* 15, no. 3 (May 2012): 398–407, https://doi.org/10.1111/j.1467-7687.2012.01142.x.

34   R. Flom and L. E. Bahrick, "The Development of Infant Discrimination of Affect in Multimodal and Unimodal Stimulation: The Role of Intersensory Redundancy," *Developmental Psychology* 43, no. 1 (2007): 238–52, https://psycnet.apa.org/doi/10.1037/0012-1649.43.1.238.

35   Tali Shenfield et al., "Maternal Singing Modulates Infant Arousal," *Psychology of Music* 31, no. 4 (October 2003): 365–75, https://doi.org/10.1177/03057356030314002.

PHYSICAL DEVELOPMENT

- **Motor Skills Development:** Engaging with musical toys, instruments, or rhythmic movement helps develop gross and fine motor skills.[36]
- **Improved Sleep Patterns:** Regular musical routines can aid in establishing sleep patterns for infants.[37]
- **Language Development:** Singing songs with infants can accelerate their acquisition of language and improve phonetic recognition.[38]
- **Increased Vocalization:** Exposure to music can encourage infants to explore their vocal cords, leading to early babbling and singing.[39]
- **Fostering Imagination and Innovation:** Music provides a fertile ground for the imagination. It encourages children to explore, experiment, and express themselves creatively. The improvisational aspect of music can particularly nurture innovative thinking and problem-solving skills.[40]

The multifaceted benefits of music education are profound and enduring, significantly enriching the early developmental stages of a child's life. It's imperative that stakeholders in education and policymaking recognize the value of music education

36 Kathleen M. Einarson and Laurel J. Trainor, "Hearing the Beat: Young Children's Perceptual Sensitivity to Beat Alignment Varies According to Metric Structure," *Music Perception* 34, no. 1 (September 2016): 56–70, https://www.jstor.org/stable/26417348.

37 Joanne Loewy et al., "The Effects of Music Therapy on Vital Signs, Feeding, and Sleep in Premature Infants," *Pediatrics* 131, no. 5 (2013): 902–918, https://doi.org/10.1542/peds.2012-1367.

38 Samuel A. Mehr et al., "For 5-Month-Old Infants, Melodies Are Social," *Psychological Science* 27, no. 4 (2016): 486–501, https://doi.org/10.1177/0956797615626691.

39 Mechthild Papoušek, "Intuitive Parenting: A Hidden Source of Musical Stimulation in Infancy," in *Musical Beginnings: Origins and Development of Musical Competence* (February 1996), 88–112.

40 Theano Koutsoupidou and David J. Hargreaves, "An Experimental Study of the Effects of Improvisation on the Development of Children's Creative Thinking in Music," *Psychology of Music* 37, no. 3 (2009): 251–78, https://doi.org/10.1177/0305735608097246.

and strive to make it accessible for every child. The harmonious blend of cognitive, creative, and emotional growth catalyzed by music education underscores its pivotal role in nurturing well-rounded, resilient, and imaginative individuals ready to embrace the challenges and opportunities of the future.

IMPACT ON YOUNG CHILDREN (FIVE TO TWELVE YEARS OLD)

Music has long been recognized as a potent force in human development and learning. For children aged five to twelve, music education can significantly contribute to their cognitive, emotional, psychological, and behavioral growth. This section explores the myriad benefits of music learning in child development, with a particular focus on neural connectivity in different brain regions.

COGNITIVE DEVELOPMENT

- **Enhanced Learning Abilities:** Music engages cognitive functions like planning, working memory, inhibition, and flexibility, known as executive functions (EF).[41] The longitudinal studies on collective music education have shown a positive trend in children's development through music over a school year, demonstrating the critical role music plays in shaping the cognitive attributes of young minds.[42]

---

41 Elisabeth Dumont et al., "Music Interventions and Child Development: A Critical Review and Further Directions," *Frontiers in Psychology* 8 (September 29, 2017): 1694, https://doi.org/10.3389/fpsyg.2017.01694.

42 Beatriz Ilari, "Longitudinal Research on Music Education and Child Development: Contributions and Challenges," *Music & Science* 3 (2020), https://doi.org/10.1177/2059204320937224; Lia Peralta, "Benefits of Music to the Brain," *Save the Music Foundation* (blog), April 4, 2018, https://www.savethemusic.org/blog/research/benefits-to-the-brain/; and Candace Nelson, "Calming, Engaging, Rewarding: How Music Can Help Mental Health with Children," Mayo Clinic Press, January 26, 2023, https://mcpress.mayoclinic.org/parenting/calming-engaging-rewarding-how-music-can-help-childrens-mental-health/.

- **Improved Mathematical Abilities:** Children engaged in music can display enhanced spatial-temporal skills, which can be foundational for understanding complex mathematical concepts.[43]
- **Better Reading Skills:** Music education can strengthen phonological processing, aiding in reading proficiency.[44]

SOCIAL DEVELOPMENT

- **Enhanced Teamwork:** Being part of a musical group or ensemble fosters cooperation, patience, and collaborative skills.[45]
- **Improved Self-Confidence:** Mastering a musical piece or instrument can bolster a child's self-esteem and sense of accomplishment.[46]

EMOTIONAL DEVELOPMENT

- **Emotional Expression and Recognition:** Children engaged in music learn to recognize, articulate, and appreciate a wide range of emotions.[47]

---

43   Frances H. Rauscher et al., "Music and Spatial Task Performance," *Nature* 365, no. 611 (1993), https://doi.org/10.1038/365611a0.

44   Sylvain Moreno et al., "Music-Learning Influences Linguistic Abilities in 8-Year-Old Children: More Evidence for Brain Plasticity," *Cerebral Cortex* 19, no. 3 (March 2009): 712–23, https://doi.org/10.1093/cercor/bhn120.

45   Sebastian Kirschner and Michael Tomasello, "Joint Music Making Promotes Prosocial Behavior in 4-Year-Old Children," *Evolution and Human Behavior* 31, no. 5 (September 2010): 354–64, https://doi.org/10.1016/j.evolhumbehav.2010.04.004.

46   Eugenia Costa-Giomi, "Effects of Three Years of Piano Instruction on Children's Academic Achievement, School Performance and Self-Esteem," *Psychology of Music* 32, no. 2 (April 2004): 139–52, https://doi.org/10.1177/0305735604041491.

47   W. F. Thompson et al., "Decoding Speech Prosody: Do Music Lessons Help?," *Emotion* 4, no. 1 (2004): 46–64, https://psycnet.apa.org/doi/10.1037/1528-3542.4.1.46.

- **Resilience and Grit:** Persisting through musical challenges can foster resilience and a "growth mindset."[48]
- **Psychological Well-Being:** Engaging in music activities can enhance self-expression, self-confidence, and self-esteem, creating a conducive environment for emotional growth and behavioral maturity.[49]
- **Emotional Competence:** Music education has been associated with enhanced emotional intelligence, which is crucial for adapting to new scenarios and fostering teamwork. These skills are vital for both the academic and social success of children.[50]

PHYSICAL DEVELOPMENT

- **Fine Motor Skill Development:** Learning instruments sharpens dexterity and fine motor skills essential for tasks outside of music.[51]
- **Enhanced Auditory Discrimination:** Continuous exposure to music strengthens the auditory system, refining the ability to process sound and discerning between subtle differences.[52]

48 Susan A. O'Neill, "Developing a Young Musician's Growth Mindset: The Role of Motivation, Self-Theories, and Resiliency," in *Music and the Mind: Essays in Honor of John Sloboda*, ed. Irène Deliège and Jane Davidson (Oxford University Press, 2011), 31–46.

49 José Salvador Blasco-Magraner et al., "Effects of the Educational Use of Music on 3- to 12-Year-Old Children's Emotional Development: A Systematic Review," *International Journal of Environmental Research and Public Health* 18, no. 7 (2021): 3668, https://doi.org/10.3390/ijerph18073668.

50 Blasco-Magraner et al., "Effects of the Educational Use of Music."

51 Marie Forgeard et al., "Practicing a Musical Instrument in Childhood Is Associated with Enhanced Verbal Ability and Nonverbal Reasoning," *PloS One* 3, no. 10 (2008): e3566, https://doi.org/10.1371/journal.pone.0003566.

52 Dana L. Strait et al., "Musical Training During Early Childhood Enhances the Neural Encoding of Speech in Noise," *Brain and Language* 123, no. 3 (December 2012): 191–201, https://doi.org/10.1016/j.bandl.2012.09.001.

- **Coordination:** A study conducted by Martins et al, high-lighted the positive impact of music education on children's coordination. Through a sustained twenty-four-week program of Orff-based music education, which included playing simple tuned percussion instruments, children exhibited improved coordination.[53]

BEHAVIORAL BENEFITS

- **Improved Concentration and Attention:** Practicing and performing music requires sustained attention, thereby enhancing focus and concentration.[54]
- **Discipline and Time Management:** Regular practice routines cultivate discipline and time management skills.[55]

IMPACT ON TEENAGERS (THIRTEEN TO NINETEEN YEARS OLD)

The adolescent years, marked by rapid cognitive, emotional, and social development, offer a fertile ground for the nurturing impact of music education. The enchanting realms of music not only fuel the artistic and creative spirits of teenagers but also significantly influence their brain development, thereby fostering a holistic growth. This section focuses on the multi-faceted benefits of music education for teenagers aged thirteen to nineteen, underscoring its pivotal role in shaping neural connectivity across diverse brain regions.

---

53   Graham F. Welch et al., "Editorial: The Impact of Music on Human Development and Well-Being," *Frontiers in Psychology* 11 (2020), https://doi.org/10.3389/fpsyg.2020.01246.

54   Hanna-Pladdy and Mackay, "The Relation Between Instrumental Musical Activity and Cognitive Aging."

55   John A. Sloboda et al., "The Role of Practice in the Development of Performing Musicians," *British Journal of Psychology* 87, no. 2 (May 1996): 287–309, https://doi.org/10.1111/j.2044-8295.1996.tb02591.x.

COGNITIVE DEVELOPMENT

- **Higher Academic Achievement:** Adolescents involved in music tend to have higher academic achievement across subjects.[56]
- **Enhanced Memory and Recall:** Music education can lead to improved verbal memory and recall capabilities.[57]
- Music education activates multiple cortical and subcortical brain areas, including the prefrontal cortex, which is closely associated with executive functions (EF) like problem-solving, planning, and attention.[58]

SOCIAL DEVELOPMENT

- **Strengthened Peer Relationships:** Being part of music groups or bands can foster deeper friendships and positive peer interactions.[59]
- **Cultural Awareness and Empathy:** Exposure to diverse musical genres can foster an appreciation for various cultures and enhance empathy.[60]

---

56 Darby E. Southgate and Vincent J. Roscigno, "The Impact of Music on Childhood and Adolescent Achievement," *Social Science Quarterly* 90, no. 1 (March 2009): 4–21, https://doi.org/10.1111/j.1540-6237.2009.00598.x.

57 Y.-C. Ho et al., "Music Training Improves Verbal but Not Visual Memory: Cross-Sectional and Longitudinal Explorations in Children," *Neuropsychology* 17, no. 3 (2003): 439–50, https://psycnet.apa.org/doi/10.1037/0894-4105.17.3.439.

58 Claudia L. R. Gonzalez et al., "Musical Training Enhances Inhibitory Control in Adolescence," in *Inhibitory Control Training: A Multidisciplinary Approach*, ed. Sara Palermo and Massimo Bartoli (2020); and Elisabeth Dumont et al., "Music Interventions and Child Development: A Critical Review and Further Directions," *Frontiers in Psychology* 8 (September 29, 2017): 1694, https://doi.org/10.3389/fpsyg.2017.01694.

59 Cecil Adderley et al., "A Home Away from Home: The World of the High School Music Classroom," *Journal of Research in Music Education* 51, no. 3 (Fall 2003): https://doi.org/10.2307/3345373.

60 Patricia Shehan Campbell, *Teaching Music Globally: Experiencing Music, Expressing Culture* (Oxford University Press, 2004).

EMOTIONAL DEVELOPMENT

- **Emotional Outlet:** Music provides teenagers a means to express complex emotions and cope with challenges.[61]
- Music is a potent emotional stimulant affecting the limbic system and prefrontal cortex, which are in the midst of development during adolescence. This interaction fosters a conducive environment for emotional and psychological growth.[62]
- **Reduction in Anxiety and Stress:** Playing, listening to, or composing music can act as a stress reliever and reduce symptoms of anxiety.[63]

PHYSICAL DEVELOPMENT

- **Improved Motor Coordination:** Advanced music learning in instruments refines motor skills and hand–eye coordination.[64]

61 Suvi Saarikallio, "Music as Emotional Self-Regulation Throughout Adulthood," *Psychology of Music* 39, no. 3 (2011): 307–327, https://doi.org/10.1177/0305735610374894.

62 Lauren Jones, "Music as an Emotional Stimulant During Puberty," *The Adolescent Brain* (blog), October 1, 2018, https://scholarblogs.emory.edu/theadolescentbrain/2018/10/01/music-as-an-emotional-stimulant-during-puberty/.

63 Mona Lisa Chanda and Daniel J. Levitin, "The Neurochemistry of Music," *Trends in Cognitive Sciences* 17, no. 4 (April 2013): 179–93, https://doi.org/10.1016/j.tics.2013.02.007.

64 Robert J. Zatorre et al., "When the Brain Plays Music: Auditory–Motor Interactions in Music Perception and Production," *Nature Reviews Neuroscience* 8 (2007): 547–58, https://doi.org/10.1038/nrn2152.

BEHAVIORAL BENEFITS

- **Enhanced Discipline and Commitment:** Rigorous music practices and performances teach teenagers the importance of dedication and perseverance.[65]
- **Reduced Risky Behaviors:** Engaging in musical activities can divert teenagers from delinquent behaviors or substance abuse.[66]

NEUROLOGICAL IMPACTS

- **Enhanced Brain Connectivity:** Music learning can lead to increased connectivity in various brain regions, especially those related to auditory processing and motor functions.[67]
- **Improved Auditory Skills:** Adolescents with music training demonstrate refined auditory skills, enabling better speech perception in noisy environments.[68]
- **Neuroplasticity:** The teenage brain undergoes significant development, and music learning can facilitate this neuroplasticity, leading to enhanced cognitive functions.[69]

---

65 Gary E. McPherson and Jane W. Davidson, "Playing an Instrument," in *The Child as Musician: A Handbook of Musical Development* (Oxford University Press, 2006), 331–51.

66 Beckett A. Broh, "Linking Extracurricular Programming to Academic Achievement: Who Benefits and Why?," *Sociology of Education* 75, no. 1 (January 2002): 69–95, https://doi.org/10.2307/3090254.

67 Gottfried Schlaug et al., "In Vivo Evidence of Structural Brain Asymmetry in Musicians," *Science* 267, no. 5198 (February 3, 1995): 699–701, https://doi.org/10.1126/science.7839149.

68 Dana L. Strait and Nina Kraus, "Biological Impact of Auditory Expertise Across the Life Span: Musicians as a Model of Auditory Learning," *Hearing Research* 308 (February 2014): 109–121, https://doi.org/10.1016/j.heares.2013.08.004.

69 Sibylle C. Herholz and Robert J. Zatorre, "Music Training as a Framework for Brain Plasticity: Behavior, Function, and Structure," *Neuron* 76, no. 3 (November 8, 2012): 486–502, https://doi.org/10.1016/j.neuron.2012.10.011.

IMPACT ON ADULTS (TWENTY TO SIXTY YEARS OLD)

The adult years are marked by significant life transitions and increasing responsibilities. The cognitive demands of adult life are substantial, requiring the ability to make critical decisions, solve problems creatively, adapt to change, and continuously learn new skills. It is in this context that the cognitive and creative benefits of music education can be profoundly valuable. By enhancing neural connectivity, improving memory, and fostering creative thinking, music learning equips adults with the mental agility and resilience needed to thrive in the face of life's complexities. Moreover, as adults look ahead to the rapid technological and societal changes on the horizon, the development of creative capability through music education becomes increasingly crucial.

COGNITIVE DEVELOPMENT

- **Enhanced Cognitive Flexibility:** Adults engaged in music may have better cognitive flexibility, allowing them to adapt to new information or environments efficiently.[70]
- **Delayed Cognitive Decline:** Musical engagement might slow the rate of cognitive decline in aging adults.[71]
- Music education can act as a potent intervention against age-related cognitive decline, by improving cognitive reserve—the brain's resilience to age-related neurodegenerative changes. It does so by engaging and strengthening various cognitive faculties such as attention, memory, and

---

70 Hanna-Pladdy and Mackay, "The Relation Between Instrumental Musical Activity and Cognitive Aging."

71 Joe Verghese et al., "Leisure Activities and the Risk of Dementia in the Elderly," *New England Journal of Medicine* 348, no. 25 (June 19, 2003): 2508–516, https://doi.org/10.1056/nejmoa022252.

self-discipline, which in turn helps in staving off cognitive impairments associated with aging.[72]

- Learning to play an instrument or sing requires the integration of sensory and motor systems, which can enhance auditory discrimination, fine motor skills, and spatial-temporal reasoning. A scoping review noted that playing a musical instrument was associated with improved cognitive health in school students, older adults, and individuals with mild brain injuries, via effects on motor, cognitive, and social processes.[73] Additionally, a report from Harvard Health states that music listeners had higher scores for mental well-being and slightly reduced levels of anxiety and depression compared to people overall.[74]

SOCIAL DEVELOPMENT

- **Strengthened Social Bonds:** Participating in group musical activities, such as choirs or bands, can strengthen social connections and counter feelings of isolation.[75]
- **Social Engagement and Emotional Well-Being:** Music education often involves social interactions, fostering empathy, cooperation, and a sense of community. Engaging in musical

---

72 Shahram Heshmat, "The Benefit of Musical Training on the Aging Brain," *Psychology Today*, August 22, 2021, https://www.psychologytoday.com/us/blog/science-choice/202108/the-benefit-musical-training-the-aging-brain.

73 Jian Sun, "Exploring the Impact of Music Education on the Psychological and Academic Outcomes of Students: Mediating Role of Self-Efficacy and Self-Esteem," *Frontiers in Psychology* 13 (February 8, 2022): 841204, https://doi.org/10.3389/fpsyg.2022.841204.

74 Andrew E. Budson, "Why Is Music Good for the Brain?," *Harvard Health Blog*, October 7, 2020, https://www.health.harvard.edu/blog/why-is-music-good-for-the-brain-2020100721062.

75 S. M. Clift and G. Hancox, "The Perceived Benefits of Singing: Findings from Preliminary Surveys of a University College Choral Society," *Perspectives in Public Health* 121, no. 4 (2001): 248–56, https://doi.org/10.1177/146642400112100409.

activities provides a platform for social engagement, which has been shown to enhance healthy aging and prolong life.[76]

- Additionally, the emotional and psychological well-being derived from musical engagement can lead to increased self-confidence, self-esteem, and a positive self-image, which in turn promotes a healthier lifestyle.[77]
- **Enhanced Communication Skills:** Music fosters a sense of shared understanding, which can positively impact interpersonal communication.[78]

EMOTIONAL DEVELOPMENT

- **Mood Regulation:** Music can act as an emotional outlet, helping in regulating mood and reducing feelings of sadness or anxiety.[79]
- **Increased Emotional Intelligence:** Engaging with diverse music genres can foster a deeper understanding and recognition of emotions.[80]

76 Heshmat, "The Benefit of Musical Training on the Aging Brain."

77 Nina Kraus and Bharath Chandrasekaran, "Music Training for the Development of Auditory Skills," *Nature Reviews Neuroscience* 11 (2010): 599–605, https://doi.org/10.1038/nrn2882.

78 Sarah C. Izen et al., "Music as a Window into Real-World Communication," *Frontiers in Psychology* 14 (2023): 1012839, https://doi.org/10.3389/fpsyg.2023.1012839.

79 Myriam V. Thoma et al., "The Effect of Music on the Human Stress Response," *PLoS ONE* 8, no. 8 (2013): e70156, https://doi.org/10.1371/journal.pone.0070156.

80 K. V. Petrides and A. Furnham, "Trait Emotional Intelligence: Behavioural Validation in Two Studies of Emotion Recognition and Reactivity to Mood Induction," *European Journal of Personality* 17, no. 1 (2003): 39–57, https://psycnet.apa.org/doi/10.1002/per.466.

BEHAVIORAL BENEFITS

- **Increased Discipline and Structure:** The regular practice and engagement with music help instill a structured routine in adults, enhancing discipline.[81]
- **Reduced Stress:** Active participation in music can act as a relaxation tool, providing a break from daily stressors.[82]
- Music has the power to evoke strong emotions and provide an escape from everyday stresses, thereby acting as a nonpharmacological intervention to combat stress and anxiety. The pleasurable experiences associated with music can induce the release of neurotransmitters like dopamine and serotonin, which are known for their roles in mood regulation and pleasure signaling.[83]

NEUROLOGICAL IMPACTS

- **Neural Plasticity:** Even in adulthood, learning an instrument or engaging deeply with music can lead to structural changes in the brain, demonstrating continued neuroplasticity.[84]
- **Improved Auditory Processing:** Continuous engagement with music refines the adult brain's auditory processing capabilities, even in noisy environments.[85]

---

81 K. A. Ericsson et al., "The Role of Deliberate Practice in the Acquisition of Expert Performance," *Psychological Review* 100, no. 3 (1993): 363–406, https://psycnet.apa.org/doi/10.1037/0033-295X.100.3.363.

82 Stéphanie Khalfa et al., "Effects of Relaxing Music on Salivary Cortisol Level After Psychological Stress," *Neurosciences and Music* 999, no. 1 (November 2003): 374–76, https://doi.org/10.1196/annals.1284.045.

83 Heshmat, "The Benefit of Musical Training on the Aging Brain."

84 Gaser and Schlaug, "Brain Structures Differ Between Musicians and Non-Musicians."

85 B. R. Zendel and C. Alain, "Musicians Experience Less Age-Related Decline in Central Auditory Processing," *Psychology and Aging* 27, no. 2 (2012): 410–17, https://psycnet.apa.org/doi/10.1037/a0024816.

- **Enhanced Memory:** Musical engagement can have a positive impact on various types of memory functions in adults.[86]

Engaging in music education during adulthood not only serves as a source of leisure and joy but also facilitates numerous cognitive, emotional, social, behavioral, and neurological benefits. It reinforces the notion that it's never too late to start a musical journey, and the positive implications of doing so are many and varied.

IMPACT ON ELDERS (SIXTY YEARS AND OLDER)

For elders aged sixty and above, music education and engagement present a unique array of advantages that contribute to healthy aging, both cognitively and emotionally. The profound impact of music education on elders transcends the mere act of making music. It offers a holistic approach to promoting cognitive, emotional, and social wellness, thereby significantly contributing to the quality of life and well-being of individuals in their golden years.

NEUROLOGICAL BENEFITS

- **Brain Plasticity Preservation:** Engaging in musical activities can help elders maintain neuroplasticity, fostering the brain's ability to change and adapt.[87]
- **Delayed Cognitive Decline:** Elders involved in music show

---

86 Michael S. Franklin et al., "The Effects of Musical Training on Verbal Memory," *Psychology of Music* 36, no. 3 (2008): 353–65, https://doi.org/10.1177/0305735607086044.

87 Catherine Y. Wan and Gottfried Schlaug, "Music Making as a Tool for Promoting Brain Plasticity Across the Life Span," *Neuroscientist* 16, no. 5 (2010): 566–77, https://doi.org/10.1177/1073858410377805.

signs of slower cognitive decline compared to their nonmusically engaged peers.[88]

- **Enhanced Auditory Processing:** Continuous engagement with music can help older adults retain better auditory processing abilities, crucial for understanding speech.[89]
- **Protection Against Dementia:** Musical activities may offer some protection against dementia and Alzheimer's disease.[90]
- Engaging in musical activities can stimulate the brain, potentially leading to the creation of new neurons, even in advanced age.[91]

BEHAVIORAL BENEFITS

- **Improved Motor Skills:** Playing an instrument can help elders maintain and even enhance their motor skills, aiding in daily tasks.[92]
- **Structured Routine:** Regular practice and musical engagement can provide elders with a structured routine, which is beneficial for cognitive health.[93]

---

88 Hanna-Pladdy and Mackay, "The Relation Between Instrumental Musical Activity and Cognitive Aging."

89 Zendel and Alain, "Musicians Experience Less Age-Related Decline in Central Auditory Processing."

90 Verghese et al., "Leisure Activities and the Risk of Dementia in the Elderly."

91 Sylvain Moreno and Gavin M. Bidelman, "Examining Neural Plasticity and Cognitive Benefit Through the Unique Lens of Musical Training," *Hearing Research* 308 (2014): 84–97, https://doi.org/10.1016/j.heares.2013.09.012.

92 J. A. Bugos et al., "Individualized Piano Instruction Enhances Executive Functioning and Working Memory in Older Adults," *Aging & Mental Health* 11, no. 4 (2007): 464–71, https://doi.org/10.1080/13607860601086504.

93 Ericsson et al., "The Role of Deliberate Practice in the Acquisition of Expert Performance."

EMOTIONAL BENEFITS

- **Emotional Resilience:** Listening to or playing music can offer emotional solace, helping elders cope with feelings of loneliness, depression, or anxiety.[94]
- Music therapy and engagement can lead to enhanced mood, potentially acting as a nonpharmacological intervention for depression in elders.[95]
- **Enhanced Quality of Life:** Engaging with music, whether listening or playing, can significantly improve the overall quality of life for elders.[96]
- Music education can also serve as a motivating activity, providing a sense of accomplishment and joy, which are essential for promoting positive psychological and behavioral outcomes among elders.[97]
- **Social Connection:** Group musical activities, such as choirs or ensemble playing, offer elders opportunities for social interaction, reducing feelings of isolation.[98]
- Listening to pleasurable music leads to the release of dopamine, the "feel-good" neurotransmitter, which plays a role in motivation, pleasure, and reward.[99]

---

94 Terrence Hays and Victor Minichiello, "The Meaning of Music in the Lives of Older People: A Qualitative Study," *Psychology of Music* 33, no. 4 (2005): 437–51, https://doi.org/10.1177/0305735605056160.

95 Agnes S. Chan et al., "Music Training Improves Verbal Memory," *Nature* 396 (1998): 128, https://doi.org/10.1038/24075.

96 Andrea Creech et al., "Active Music Making: A Route to Enhanced Subjective Well-Being Among Older People," *Perspectives in Public Health* 133, no. 1 (2013): 36–43, https://doi.org/10.1177/1757913912466950.

97 Teppo Särkämö et al., "Music Listening Enhances Cognitive Recovery and Mood After Middle Cerebral Artery Stroke," *Brain* 131, no. 3 (March 2008): 866–76, https://doi.org/10.1093/brain/awn013; and Sofia Seinfeld et al., "Effects of Music Learning and Piano Practice on Cognitive Function, Mood and Quality of Life in Older Adults," *Frontiers in Psychology* 4 (2013): 810, https://doi.org/10.3389/fpsyg.2013.00810.

98 Simon Coulton et al., "Effectiveness and Cost-Effectiveness of Community Singing on Mental Health-Related Quality of Life of Older People: Randomised Controlled Trial," *British Journal of Psychiatry* 207, no. 3 (2015): 250–55, https://doi.org/10.1192/bjp.bp.113.129908.

99 Valorie N. Salimpoor et al., "Anatomically Distinct Dopamine Release During Anticipation and Experience of Peak Emotion to Music," *Nature Neuroscience* 14 (2011): 257–62, https://doi.org/10.1038/nn.2726.

POTENTIAL PROTECTIVE BENEFITS

- **Stimulating Multiple Brain Regions:** Music, being a complex auditory input, activates various brain regions, helping in their maintenance and function.[100]
- **Musical "Exercise" for the Brain:** Just as physical exercise benefits the body, learning and playing music act as an exercise for the brain, potentially slowing down its aging process.[101]

ENHANCED MEMORY RETRIEVAL

- Music can serve as a mnemonic device, aiding in the recall of memories, especially for those with Alzheimer's or dementia.[102]

IMPROVED EXECUTIVE FUNCTIONS

- Elders involved in regular musical activities often display improved executive functions like problem-solving, task switching, and information processing.[103]

---

100 Stefan Koelsch, "A Neuroscientific Perspective on Music Therapy," *Neurosciences and Music III Disorders and Plasticity* 1169, no. 1 (July 2009): 374–84, https://doi.org/10.1111/j.1749-6632.2009.04592.x.

101 Hanna-Pladdy and Mackay, "The Relation Between Instrumental Musical Activity and Cognitive Aging."

102 Jörn-Henrik Jacobsen et al., "Why Musical Memory Can Be Preserved in Advanced Alzheimer's Disease," *Brain* 138, no. 8 (August 2015): 2438–50, https://doi.org/10.1093/brain/awv135.

103 Brenda Hanna-Pladdy and Byron Gajewski, "Recent and Past Musical Activity Predicts Cognitive Aging Variability: Direct Comparison with General Lifestyle Activities," *Frontiers in Human Neuroscience* 6 (July 19, 2012): 198, https://doi.org/10.3389/fnhum.2012.00198.

DELAY IN AGE-RELATED HEARING LOSS

- Musicians often display better auditory abilities, and their training may delay age-related hearing loss.[104]

PROTECTION AGAINST STRESS AND RELATED DISORDERS

- Music can lower cortisol levels, potentially protecting elders from disorders related to chronic stress.[105]

ENHANCING SPATIAL-TEMPORAL SKILLS

- Learning and playing musical instruments can boost spatial-temporal skills, which are essential for tasks like planning, organization, and visual discernment.[106]

PRESERVATION OF SPEECH PROCESSING

- Music learning can enhance the neural encoding of speech, aiding in better comprehension, especially in noisy environments.[107]

104 Alexandra Parbery-Clark et al., "Musical Experience and the Aging Auditory System: Implications for Cognitive Abilities and Hearing Speech in Noise," *PloS One* 6, no. 5 (2011): e18082, https://doi.org/10.1371/journal.pone.0018082.

105 Daisy Fancourt et al., "The Psychoneuroimmunological Effects of Music: A Systematic Review and a New Model," *Brain, Behavior, and Immunity* 36 (February 2014): 15–26, https://doi.org/10.1016/j.bbi.2013.10.014.

106 Gaser and Schlaug, "Brain Structures Differ Between Musicians and Non-Musicians."

107 Strait and Kraus, "Biological Impact of Auditory Expertise Across the Life Span."

REDUCED RISK OF STROKE AND FASTER RECOVERY

- Engaging in musical activities can potentially reduce the risk of stroke and aid in faster recovery by improving neural connections.[108]

DEMENTIA, ALZHEIMER'S DISEASE, AGE-RELATED BRAIN DETERIORATION

The profound impact of music on the senior brain underscores the potential of musical interventions as both preventive and rehabilitative measures against age-related cognitive decline. Engaging with music in various forms can be a potent tool for promoting a healthy and active aging process.

STRENGTHENING THE AUDITORY SYSTEM

- Regular exposure to music can enhance the auditory system, making it more resilient against age-related changes.[109]

ENHANCED MULTISENSORY INTEGRATION

- Musicians often develop better multisensory integration, which may help in preserving this function during aging.[110]

---

108 Eckart Altenmüller and Gottfried Schlaug, "Apollo's Gift: New Aspects of Neurologic Music Therapy," *Progress in Brain Research* 217 (2015): 237–52, https://doi.org/10.1016/bs.pbr.2014.11.029.

109 A. Parbery-Clark et al., "Context-Dependent Encoding in the Auditory Brainstem Subserves Enhanced Speech-in-Noise Perception in Musicians," *Neuropsychologia* 49, no. 12 (October 2011): 3338–45, https://doi.org/10.1016/j.neuropsychologia.2011.08.007.

110 Karin Petrini et al., "Multisensory Integration of Drumming Actions: Musical Expertise Affects Perceived Audiovisual Asynchrony," *Experimental Brain Research* 198 (2009): 339–52, https://psycnet.apa.org/doi/10.1007/s00221-009-1817-2.

IMPROVED COGNITIVE FLEXIBILITY

- Music learning can enhance cognitive flexibility, aiding in better task switching and adaptability.[111]

PROTECTION AGAINST COGNITIVE DECLINE

- Engaging in musical activities can delay cognitive decline, offering protection against dementia and Alzheimer's.[112]

EMOTIONAL REGULATION AND STRESS REDUCTION

- Music can promote emotional regulation, offering therapeutic effects for dementia patients.[113]

IMPROVED MEMORY AND RECALL

- Music can facilitate better memory encoding, crucial for Alzheimer's patients.[114]

PRESERVATION OF LANGUAGE SKILLS

- Music learning can enhance the neural encoding of speech, aiding in the preservation of language skills.[115]

---

111 Sylvain Moreno et al., "Short-Term Music Training Enhances Verbal Intelligence and Executive Function," *Psychological Science* 22, no. 11 (2011): 1425–33, https://doi.org/10.1177/0956797611416999.

112 Hanna-Pladdy and Mackay, "The Relation Between Instrumental Musical Activity and Cognitive Aging."

113 Thoma et al., "The Effect of Music on the Human Stress Response."

114 Petr Janata, "The Neural Architecture of Music-Evoked Autobiographical Memories," *Cerebral Cortex* 19, no. 11 (November 2009): 2579–94, https://doi.org/10.1093/cercor/bhp253.

115 Patrick C. M. Wong, "Musical Experience Shapes Human Brainstem Encoding of Linguistic Pitch Patterns," *Nature Neuroscience* 10 (2007): 420–22, https://doi.org/10.1038/nn1872.

INCREASED BRAIN RESILIENCE

- Playing a musical instrument engages various brain regions, building redundancy, which may delay the onset of dementia symptoms.[116]

MOTOR SKILLS AND COORDINATION

- Playing an instrument promotes motor skills, potentially slowing the decline of motor functions in neurodegenerative diseases.[117]

SOCIAL ENGAGEMENT AND DECREASED ISOLATION

- Group musical activities can foster social bonds, crucial for mental health and combating feelings of isolation common in dementia patients.[118]

PROMOTION OF NEUROPLASTICITY

- Continuous musical learning can induce changes in brain structure and function, promoting neuroplasticity.[119]

---

116 Altenmüller and Schlaug, "Apollo's Gift: New Aspects of Neurologic Music Therapy."

117 Catherine Y. Wan and Gottfried Schlaug, "Neural Pathways for Language in Autism: The Potential for Music-Based Treatments," *Future Neurology* 5, no. 6 (2010): 797–805, https://doi.org/10.2217/fnl.10.55.

118 Creech et al., "Active Music Making."

119 Herholz and Zatorre, "Music Training as a Framework for Brain Plasticity."

MUSIC AS NONPHARMACOLOGICAL INTERVENTION

- Music therapy can act as a nonpharmacological intervention, reducing the need for medications in managing behavioral and psychological symptoms in dementia.[120]

120 Alfredo Raglio et al., "Efficacy of Music Therapy in the Treatment of Behavioral and Psychiatric Symptoms of Dementia," *Alzheimer Disease & Associated Disorders* 22, no. 2 (April 2008): 158–62, https://doi.org/10.1097/wad.0b013e3181630b6f.